THE REAL READER'S

Slightly Foxed

'Jocelin's Folly'

NO.71   AUTUMN 2021

Editors Gail Pirkis & Hazel Wood
Marketing and publicity Stephanie Allen & Jennie Harrison Bunning
Bookshops Anna Kirk
Subscriptions Hattie Summers & Jess Dalby

Cover illustration: Jackie Morris, *Spring into Autumn*, watercolour and gold leaf

Jackie Morris, born in 1961, grew up with a desire to paint. She studied art at Bath Academy of Art and has exhibited her work internationally. She is the illustrator of many books and the author of some. In 2019 *The Lost Words*, a book made in collaboration with Robert Macfarlane, won the Greenaway Medal. Her inspiration is found between the feathers of a raven's wing in flight, in the voices of birds, the turning of the year and the shape of a fox. Books, art, paint, creativity, poetry, the remnant boxes of antique paints, all these things and more are an inspiration. She also has a passion for old typewriters, the songs they sing and their scent. Her work is represented by Jessica Woollard (agent) and Seven Fables, Dulverton (paintings, books, prints).

Design by Octavius Murray
Layout by Andrew Evans
Colophon and tailpiece by David Eccles

Published by Slightly Foxed Limited
53 Hoxton Square
London N1 6PB

tel 020 7033 0258
email office@foxedquarterly.com
www.foxedquarterly.com

Slightly Foxed is published quarterly in early March, June, September and December

Annual subscription rates (4 issues)
UK and Ireland £48; Overseas £56

Single copies of this issue can be bought for £12.50 (UK) or £14.50 (Overseas)

All back issues in printed form are also available

ISBN 978-1-910898-62-8
ISSN 1742-5794

Printed and bound by Smith Settle, Yeadon, West Yorkshire

Contents

From the Editors 5

Jocelin's Folly · ANDREW JOYNES
William Golding, *The Spire* 7

Elegy to a Family · PATRICK WELLAND
George Clare, *Last Waltz in Vienna* 13

A Down-to-Earth Visionary · MARGARET DRABBLE
Doris Lessing, *The Four-Gated City* 19

Paper Trails · CHARLES ELLIOTT
Richard Altick, *The Scholar Adventurers* 24

Plenty to Say · OLIVIA POTTS
The novels of Mary Wesley 28

Gone Fishing · ADAM SISMAN
Hugh Falkus, *The Stolen Years* 34

Magical Talisman · SUE GAISFORD
Rosemary Sutcliff, *Sword Song* & *The Shield Ring* 39

The Ubiquitous Canadian · MICHAEL BARBER
Charles Ritchie, *The Siren Years* 43

A Smooth Man in a Trilby · CLARISSA BURDEN
Josephine Tey's Inspector Grant novels 49

Dreaming of Cheese · JOHN SMART
John Squire (ed.), *Cheddar Gorge* 54

Contents

A Strangulation of the Soul · MAGGIE FERGUSSON
Brian Masters, *Killing for Company* 60

The Price of Virtue · FRANCES DONNELLY
Anita Brookner, *Hotel du Lac* 65

The Tolkien Test · KEN HAIGH
J. R. R. Tolkien, *The Hobbit* 69

Winston and Clementine · JANE RIDLEY
Mary Soames (ed.), *Speaking for Themselves* 73

Innocent or Not? · CHRISTIAN TYLER
Rita Monaldi & Francesco Sorti, *Imprimatur* 79

Out with the Galloping Major · CAROLINE JACKSON
Somerville and Ross, *Some Experiences of an Irish RM* 84

Poetry, My Mother and Me · RACHEL KELLY
The consolation of poetry 90

Bibliography 95

John Watson

The Slightly Foxed Podcast

A new episode of our podcast is available on the 15th of every month. To listen, visit www.foxedquarterly.com/pod or search for Slightly Foxed on Audioboom, iTunes or your podcast app.

Subscriber Benefits

Slightly Foxed can obtain any books reviewed in this issue, whether new or second-hand. To enquire about a book, to access the digital edition of *Slightly Foxed* or to view a list of membership benefits, visit www.foxedquarterly.com/members or contact the office: 020 7033 0258/office@foxedquarterly.com.

From the Editors

For many of us, the summer of 2021 will be remembered through the words of a song from forty years ago. 'Should I stay or should I go?' was the theme of days in which we packed and unpacked our bags, anxiously scanning the headlines. Whether in the end you decided on a staycation or ventured further afield, we hope you were refreshed by a change of scene.

As for us, we're finally back in the office and delighted to be able to see one another again. And we're looking forward to a very busy autumn!

This month we're reissuing the last two books in Rosemary Sutcliff's magnificent sequence of Roman and post-Roman novels (see p.39). In *Sword Song* the action moves to the north-west coast and the Hebrides as we sail in a longship with a young Norwegian who has a lot to learn. Two hundred years later, in *The Shield Ring*, we meet his descendant in the Lakeland hills where the Vikings are still holding out against Norman invaders. These two books are just as compelling as Sutcliff's earlier titles which, if you haven't already discovered them, are still available.

Our new Slightly Foxed Edition is George Clare's *Last Waltz in Vienna* (see p.13). Born Georg Klaar, Clare grew up in what was once the cosmopolitan capital of the Austro-Hungarian Empire, a city in which his own loving family of Jewish doctors and bankers had long thrived. But the First World War had reduced it greatly, breeding fear and resentment, and in 1938 the *Anschluss* marked the absorption of Austria into Germany. Within five years 65,000 Viennese Jews had been deported to the camps, among them Clare's own parents. This vigorous, compassionate memoir offers stark lessons for our own uneasily shared world.

Closer to home are two delightful new books, neither of which could be more English. We know many of you have enjoyed Adrian Bell's rural trilogy *Corduroy, Silver Ley* and *The Cherry Tree*, published as Slightly Foxed Editions. Now, in what we hope will be a series of Bell's seasonal essays, we're offering *A Countryman's Winter Notebook*, a selection of his much-loved columns published between 1950 and 1980 in the *Eastern Daily Press*. Filled with wisdom and humour, these are beautifully paced observations of country life with all the power of poetry – 'dark sodden fields and bright flying leaves' – but rooted in cherished everyday objects and incidents. Introduced by Richard Hawking, with a preface by Adrian's son Martin Bell, our edition is decorated with illustrations by Suffolk artist Beth Knight and would make a perfect Christmas present. It's published on 12 October.

On 9 November we're publishing another irresistible book, *Letters to Michael*. Between 1945 and 1947 Charles Phillipson wrote 150 illustrated letters to his young son. In them he captures the delight to be found in the detail of everyday life, seen through the lens of his own quirky imagination: passengers on the morning train hidden behind newspapers; the fun to be had on a revolving office chair; the different ways in which men carry their umbrellas; a walk on a very windy day; the sun rising over chimneypots; the postman on his bicycle. Jotted on rough office paper, each letter was embellished with a hand-drawn stamp which made young Michael feel as if he was receiving 'real' letters. And real letters they are – love-letters, even – for through their affectionate words, mischievous drawings and gentle encouragement, a father's love for his son shines out.

You'll find more about both books in the catalogue slipped into this issue. Meantime, we thank you, dear readers, from the bottom of our hearts for all the loyalty you've shown us in these difficult times.

GAIL PIRKIS & HAZEL WOOD

Jocelin's Folly

ANDREW JOYNES

Across the east end of the nave of Canterbury Cathedral, where I was a volunteer guide for over a decade, there is a stone strainer arch erected by Prior Thomas Goldstone 500 years ago. It is a kind of tie-bar, one of six which bind together the columns that support Bell Harry Tower, the cathedral's dominant feature. The arch is essential to the integrity of the building's central structure and is decorated with flowered designs and an inscription. On either side of the Prior's initials and his rebus – three golden pebbles, a visual pun on his surname – there is the first verse of the psalm that begins *Non nobis Domine* ('Not unto us, O Lord, but unto thy name give glory . . .').

In this way Prior Goldstone acquired a double helping of renown. He has been advertised down the centuries – on a kind of prominent stone billboard – both as the patron of a striking architectural achievement and as the humble instrument of God's intentions for His great church. During the so-called Age of Faith before the Reformation, pious self-deprecation could also mean tacit self-congratulation.

When I took groups of visitors round the cathedral, I would often refer to the motivation of the great ecclesiastical patrons like Thomas Goldstone. And I would sometimes suggest that those interested should get hold of a copy of William Golding's novel *The Spire* (1964) whose protagonist Dean Jocelin embarks, like Prior Goldstone, on a quest for personal renown through divine favour by obsessively driving forward an architectural project. Jocelin's intention is to have a

William Golding, *The Spire* (1964)
Faber · Pb · 272pp · £8.99 · ISBN 9780571307821

great spire built above his cathedral. In the end the endeavour will destroy him.

Although Golding does not identify the cathedral about which he is writing, it is generally thought to be Salisbury, where he taught at a grammar school in the cathedral close for a decade and a half from the late 1940s (his observation of the boys' playground behaviour is said to have inspired his early novel *Lord of the Flies*). Salisbury Cathedral has the tallest spire in the country – 404 feet high – and when its first incarnation was built in the fourteenth century there must have been the same sense of disquiet within the cathedral community – mutters about overweening pride and dark references to the Tower of Babel – that the fictional Dean Jocelin encounters at the outset of the novel. Jocelin is never off-stage, and every development in the plot is filtered through his frame of mind, from ecstatic exultation at curtain-up to self-doubt by the interval and eventually to despair and madness at the finale. He is taken to a very high place and is cast down, and the ascent and fall are to a large extent of his own making.

From the outset, Golding makes it clear that the presence of the masons building Jocelin's spire is disrupting the smooth order of the cathedral. The removal of walls changes the devotional nature of the building's interior, and even the Dean is aware that, until the spire on which he has set his heart has been built, the change will be for the worse.

> Facing that barricade of wood and canvas I could think this was some sort of pagan temple; and those two men posed so centrally in the sun dust with their crowbars were the priests of some outlandish rite . . .

The masons pitilessly bully one of the cathedral's sweepers, and when the Dean remonstrates with the master builder, he is told that this is their way of warding off bad luck. They down tools on the pre-Christian Midsummer Night feast, and their celebratory fires burn on the hills surrounding the city. 'They are dangerous men, strange creatures from every end of the world, and seem willing to resort to violence at the slightest provocation . . .'

It is Jocelin's relationship with Roger Mason the master builder that provides the pivot – almost like one of the masons' engineering devices – around which the novel's plot turns. At first the builder, conscious that nothing on the scale of the spire has been attempted before, is contemptuous of the cleric's insistence that faith will be sufficient to drive the project forward. He has the caution of a practical man, setting out his plumb lines and saucers of water to detect any buckling of the supporting pillars under the increasing weight of the spire as it rises. There is an extraordinary scene where the two men, surrounded by labourers and clerics and townspeople, peer into the enormous pit which has been dug at the centre of the crossing to strengthen the pillars' foundations. The rainwater is rising; there is a stench of rotting graves; and as lighted candles are lowered into the pit it can be seen that the earth itself is moving under the weight of the spire: 'some form of life, that which ought not to be seen or touched, the darkness under the earth, turning, seething, coming to the boil . . .'

Roger wants to abandon the project at this point, but for some time the Dean has been aware that the master builder is in love with the cathedral sweeper's wife. He has not spoken out against this, as a devout churchman should have done, because he realizes this is a way of putting pressure on the man ('She will keep him here . . .'). On wooden scaffolding high in the air, as the ravens swoop and croak around them, as the stones at the base of the spire vibrate eerily, 'singing' under the pressure of the weight bearing down upon them, and as the pinnacles and glass and metal of the nearly completed spire sway in the wind, the two men confront each other. Eventually Jocelin's will prevails. 'So he began to climb down the ladders with his angel; and before he was out of sight he heard Roger Mason speaking softly. "I believe you're the devil. The devil himself" . . .'

The spire continues to rise, but Jocelin's world falls. He suffers from a deterioration of the spine, a cancer perhaps, which until now has given him a sense that a supernatural being is standing just behind him, willing him on. Now the angel at his back becomes a debilitating fire. His opponents in the cathedral chapter, alarmed at the Dean's heedless persistence with an increasingly expensive and dangerous project, have made representations to Rome, and a Papal Visitor arrives to investigate. Most damaging of all to Jocelin's self-esteem, it emerges that he owes his high ecclesiastical position not to his innate ability or to divine favour, but to an act of nepotism. Though he does not know it, his well-connected aunt was once the mistress of the king, who as patron of the cathedral granted her request for a senior position for her nephew: 'We shall drop a plum in his mouth.' The rest of the cathedral chapter know of this connection, which explains the reserve bordering on contempt with which they treat their Dean from the start of the novel.

The Visitor removes Jocelin from office. He becomes a non-person. Once, in the early days of his building project, he had planned to have a sculpted head-and-shoulders image of himself placed at each of the four corners of the crossing which support the spire. He would be depicted in the guise of an angel, long hair streaming behind him in the celestial wind: thus, like Prior Goldstone at Canterbury, he would be advertised down the centuries as the God-favoured patron of a great architectural work. Now the fallen Dean does indeed have long hair, but it is straggling and uncombed. He is a wild-eyed, forlorn figure, and there is no angelic radiance in his careworn face. Even on his deathbed, he asks repeatedly about the building work. Has the spire fallen? There is a smile from the kindly chaplain whom Jocelin used to treat so condescendingly in his glory-days. 'Not yet,' he replies.

The Spire is a complex book, and it challenges the complacent assumption that the great cathedrals arose because of the simple religious faith of their builders. In the so-called Age of Faith the motivation of the grand ecclesiastical patrons contained quite as much egoism and ambition – and debate about their favoured projects contained quite as much back-biting and malice – as would be the case in our own rootless times.

When I was at a training session for Canterbury guides some years ago, I was told a story about cathedral tourism. A young priest at Salisbury was confronted late one summer afternoon by an elderly American lady who was clearly at the end of her sightseeing tether. The 'Cotswolds and Back' excursion from London had made for a very long day, and as she staggered into the sunlit nave, beneath the highest cathedral spire in England, she asked with a weary desperation, 'Is this Stonehenge?'

Then, soon after I became a guide, a young mother came into Canterbury Cathedral with a child in a pushchair. She told me that ever since he could stand up in his cot, little Ernest had looked out of his bedroom window at the cathedral's Bell Harry Tower. He was fascinated by its spires and pinnacles, glimpsed far away across the rooftops. Between them, mother and son contrived a bedtime story about the cathedral. It was, they concluded, a magical creature of great power and beauty – a Big Friendly Dragon, perhaps – which long ago settled in the city and brought good fortune to its people. Now, on a winter's afternoon, the mother had brought her child into the darkened nave to visit the BFD for the first time. The child looked around excitedly, and the flickering light of the candles reflected in his eyes.

To me, these are endearing stories. They express the 'otherness' of a great cathedral as it is perceived today, and as it is presented in William Golding's subtle and instructive novel. Whether it is seen as a mystical assembly of stone with an aura of antiquity, as a fabled creature in a bedtime story, or as an example of enduring cultural endeavour – serving perhaps as a reprimand to our restless and inattentive times – the thought of the medieval cathedral continues to loom over the modern imagination, much as the dominating vision of his spire did over the deathbed of Dean Jocelin. A cathedral used to be regarded as a kind of ark, a place of power and refuge. Has that essential idea of a great cathedral fallen? Not entirely, perhaps. 'Not yet.'

ANDREW JOYNES estimates that during his time as a guide he conducted some 6,000 visitors round Canterbury Cathedral. He suggests that studying the Middle Ages is like reversing a telescope: the entire scene appears in miniature; the figures are sharply delineated; and their relationship to each other can be precisely and easily traced.

Elegy to a Family

PATRICK WELLAND

I have a photo of Aunt Margaret standing outside Vienna's Hofburg Palace, beret jauntily askew. It is 1937 and, aged 28, she is on her return with a friend from Czechoslovakia, travelling in an Austin Ruby. Margaret – think Joyce Grenfell in *St Trinian's* – always maintained she crossed Central Europe without difficulty despite losing her passport. It seems improbable but maybe not impossible. Regardless, the small black-and-white image enduringly appeals because it was taken amid perilous events in Austria of which Margaret, in her artless exuberance for life, was probably unaware. I wanted to know more of that time.

Vienna fascinates. In its *fin-de-siècle* pomp it was not only the centre of the sprawling Austro-Hungarian Hapsburg Empire but also the most cultured city in Europe. Reduced by the First World War to being the unhappy capital of a small country riven by political violence, in 1937 it was only months from Hitler's *Anschluss*. Less than five years later, in the one-time home of such Jewish giants of literature and philosophy as Joseph Roth, Stefan Zweig and Ludwig Wittgenstein, Austria's Reich Governor Baldur von Schirach hailed his own 'contribution to European culture': the 'joyous cleansing' of Vienna through the deportation of 65,000 Jews to the camps. For a witness to what Zweig called in his *Memoirs of Yesterday* 'the most terrible defeat of reason and the most savage triumph of brutality in the chronicles of time' we can turn to George Clare and his *Last Waltz in Vienna*.

Last Waltz was first published in English in 1981, with the subtitle *The Destruction of a Family, 1842–1942*. However, the subtitle is misleading and absent from the 2007 edition. For although Clare's family's destination is horrific, his memoir is as much an elegy to the vitality of a Jewish family in a vanished age as a record of its descent to annihilation. In revealing its humanity – sometimes noble, sometimes flawed – and in detailing its joys and pains, he makes us aware of the individual lives masked by too familiar statistics of genocide. It is a story poignant enough to bring tears to the eyes.

Clare was born Georg Klaar in 1920 into a divide at the heart of pre-war Central European Jewry: between those who embraced assimilation and those who clung more tenaciously to their Jewish identity. The Klaars had risen from the ghettoes of Bukovina, straddling present-day Ukraine and Romania, to become proud citizens of the country they loved. They were Austrians of the Jewish faith. In contrast Georg's maternal family, the Immerdauers and Schapiras, were Galician Jews rooted by history and geography in orthodoxy. They were Jews who lived in Austria.

The two strains merge in the marriage of Georg's father, Ernst, to Stella Schapira in November 1919. Ernst, a senior bank accountant and a stern but loving parent, is a lover of Goethe, Schiller and Rilke, and is passionately interested in objets d'art and paintings; gentle Stella, governed more by reason than emotion, adores Dickens and Galsworthy. Their life is one of bourgeois respectability: hosting dinner parties for intellectual friends at their flat in Pichlergasse, going to the theatre to see the comedies of Franz Molnar and taking holidays in Bad Ischl, a favourite haunt of leading Austrian writers and actors.

Nearby, Georg's grandmother Julie Klaar receives visitors in her gaslit sitting-room which has not changed since the time of Emperor Franz-Josef. She has entirely shed her Eastern roots and reigns as family sovereign over her children: Ernst, Uncle Paul, a GP and gynaecologist, chain-smoking Uncle Fritz – a jobless, moustachioed former army captain looking like a figure from a Lehár operetta – Uncle Joseph and home-loving Aunt Sally, who is gently steered into marrying a regrettably impotent concert pianist.

Grandfather Bernhard Schapira and his formidable wife Adele live in grander style in the Turkenschanzplatz district. With his gold pince-nez, expensive suits and 'masterful composure' Bernhard, a wealthy member of the Stock Exchange who is chauffeured in an expensive Adler car, has all the pomposity of a grand seigneur. But, unlike the Klaars, the family observe their religion and Adele's Yiddish-accented German betrays her roots in the ghettoes of Eastern Europe.

How secure it all appears to only child Georg. At home, he feels enfolded in such love that he has the 'utter certainty that no evil

could reach me'. In cafés, matrons enjoying a life of elegant futility gossip over whipped cream coffees and cloying pastries. The Burgtheater and Konzerthaus still play to packed galleries, recalling happier imperial times. But beneath this smug veneer of *Gemütlichkeit*, and away from the imposing mansions along the Ringstrasse, lie poverty and despair. Thousands of the city's children live close to starvation, inflation and unemployment are rampant, and back streets are littered with refuse combed by the homeless. 'Behind the baroque masonry lay dark, dank corridors filled with the stale smell of over-boiled cabbage and the indefinable but clearly discernible odour of hatred and envy.' Austria is about to erupt.

Writing with restrained pathos and the authority of a first-hand witness, Clare takes us through the political and social collapse of a nation. It is an enthralling and terrible drama whose momentous events – the failed Nazi putsch of 1934, the murder of Chancellor Dollfuss, the increasingly futile political attempts by his successor Kurt von Schuschnigg to stem Hitler's ambitions – have all the inevitability of a Greek tragedy as Austria stumbles towards nemesis.

But for young Georg these history-shaping events are merely the backdrop to the small dramas of his own life. More important are visits to relatives, hiking holidays, a trip to Prague where he gets drunk for the first time and, of course, inevitable teenage rows as his growing independence clashes with paternal authoritarianism. At school, occasional anti-Semitic jokes directed at Jewish pupils by their peers are delivered more in mocking humour than malice. There are thugs on the street, but they ignore Georg. Above all, there are the joys of romance with girlfriend Lisl, later to become Georg's wife. It was 'the only taste I ever had of what it means to be young and carefree and in love with love'.

By late 1937, however, the atmosphere in the city has become so toxic that it cannot be ignored even by the self-absorption of youth. In December that year, Georg and Lisl are at Vienna's most famous satirical cabaret, the Simplicissimus. With the rest of the largely Jewish audience they briefly forget their concerns, 'all of us behaving as if we had not a care in the world'. It is only later that Georg understands that the jokes of the Jewish comedians Farkas and Grünbaum are freighted with an 'almost prophetic awareness of the menace suffusing the very air we breathed'.

Yet even as the skies darken, Georg still feels that 'everything was possible, that I was special somehow and life was about to begin'. Only three months later his naïve optimism is extinguished when the Germans march in, predators welcomed as saviours. *Last Waltz* moves from the dusk into the dark.

Clare remembers the day Austria surrendered to Hitler with awful clarity. Moments after Schuschnigg announces on the radio his nation's capitulation, the Klaars hear the shouts of hundreds of men outside. They switch off the lights and gaze out on Nussdorferstrasse as frenzied Nazis pass below in a stream of swastika-draped lorries:

Ein volk, ein Reich, ein Führer! they were chanting in chorus, followed by *Ju-da verr-rrecke! Ju-da verr-rrecke!* (Perish Judah!) . . .

coming from a thousand throats, screaming it out in the full fury of their hate . . . it is a sound one can never forget.

After they leave, Georg looks out and sees a policeman wearing a swastika armband beating a man at his feet with a truncheon. He has known that policeman all his life, seen him salute his father and befriend the family. 'Yesterday's protector had been transformed into tomorrow's persecutor and tormentor. Nothing could have driven home more clearly what had happened on this one day.' By the next afternoon, Jews are being rounded up for street cleaning in front of jeering mobs.

Scenting the Nazi stench blowing from Germany, many of Vienna's wealthier and savvier Jews have already fled the country. Ernst, indeed, is so concerned at the swelling tide of anti-Semitism that in 1938 he toys with moving the family to Switzerland. But like thousands of other Jews he decides to stay, believing the crisis will blow over. How, we ask with hindsight, could so many have been so delusional? It was, says Clare, a collective act of 'self-induced blindness'. To the end, these people so strongly and proudly absorbed into Austrian society refused to believe that the nation they loved, and for which many had fought, would turn on them. 'How could they foresee the bestialities that were to be committed in the name of the country so dear to them? How could anyone?'

The illusion brutally exposed, flight now becomes imperative and the final hundred pages of *Last Waltz* are both gripping and heart-breaking. We know that Georg will find freedom and ultimately serve in the British Army. His sinuous road to a new life, involving daunting obstacles and the threat of capture by the Gestapo, takes him from Vienna to Berlin, Latvia and Ireland before he finds sanctuary in England. We know, too, that his parents, like most of his wider family, will not survive. Their own route takes them to France where, after living in Paris and Marseilles, they are forced by the Vichy government to move to St Pierreville, a mountain village in the

Ardèche, and placed under house arrest. In 1942, Ernst is arrested. Stella, who has met the challenge of their desolated lives with greater fortitude than her husband, steadfastly refuses to leave his side. They vanish from the outside world into the awful anonymity of the camps.

There is one last family sighting. The later edition of *Last Waltz* closes with a letter written by Uncle Paul who in 1945 returned to Vienna, 'burnt out and guilt-ridden', from the Theresienstadt ghetto. Here, he reveals, he was reunited with his mother Julie who died in his arms whispering, 'I never knew dying could be that hard.' Ernst and Stella's fate is unknown.

In a world saturated with reminiscences of that terrible time, *Last Waltz* remains a unique chronicle that deserves to be read and whose message still resonates. It gives us three stories: the intimate record of a boy growing up embraced by love in a time of hate; a study of how a civilized society can fatally fracture under the weight of its own divisions and insecurities; and, finally, an examination of that oldest and most poisonous of mankind's prejudices, anti-Semitism. In the words of the historian Edward Crankshaw: 'Clare leads us gently, but inexorably, to the edge of the pit and then leaves us to look down into it.'

PATRICK WELLAND is a retired national newspaper journalist. He regrets that he was born too late to enjoy a life of elegant futility in late nineteenth-century Vienna.

George Clare's *Last Waltz in Vienna* (408pp) is now available in a limited and numbered cloth-bound edition of 2,000 copies (subscribers: UK & Eire £17, Overseas £19; non-subscribers: UK & Eire £18.50, Overseas £20.50). All prices include post and packing. Copies may be ordered by post (53 Hoxton Square, London N1 6PB), by phone (020 7033 0258) or via our website www.foxedquarterly.com.

A Down-to-Earth Visionary

MARGARET DRABBLE

I read Doris Lessing's *The Four-Gated City* in 1969, when it was published, and I have a hardback first edition of it, still in its original dust wrapper. When I rediscovered my copy and reread it in the autumn of 2019, to prepare for a seminar at the University of East Anglia to celebrate her centenary, I found that I had been using a bus ticket as a bookmark. I must have been reading it on the No. 24 bus, on my way to or from South End Green in Hampstead. I had forgotten what London bus tickets looked like. The printing was a pale mauve. I couldn't read that volume on a bus now. It is far too heavy. I can hardly read it in bed.

Lessing would have been fascinated by the pandemic. This novel is the last in her five-volume sequence *Children of Violence* which traces the fortunes of her protagonist Martha Quest from her upbringing in Southern Africa to her arrival in 1950 in England, not long after the Second World War. *The Four-Gated City* opens in the dreary bombed landscape and rationed food of 1950s London and moves on through the extreme sexual experimentation of the liberated Sixties to an apocalyptic future of poison gas, Porton Down, World War Three and bare survival. It spans a vast historical stretch, and encompasses a large cast of characters from all ranges and ages of English social life, and from several ethnicities – dockers, Jewish refugees, communists, Old Etonians, intellectuals, African politicians, trades unionists, writers, actors, disturbed adolescents, spies, psychiatrists and servants.

Doris Lessing, *The Four-Gated City* (1969)
Harper Perennial · Pb · 672pp · £13 · ISBN 9780060976675

Lessing is not afraid of the word 'servant', as some middle-class English writers are: she addresses 'the servant question' frontally, reminding us that in the Fifties the middle classes found servants 'plentiful and cheap'. It's strange to look back on this now, but it was indeed so: child-minders and cleaners cost a few pounds a week. The bohemian and vagabond Martha finds herself a position as a kind of housekeeper, personal assistant and cook for an English writer, Mark, who lives in a square in Bloomsbury, in the heart of old cultural London: she becomes deeply involved with him, his demented and hallucinating wife, and his entire family.

One of the salient 'servant' passages occurs when Martha's unhappy, problematic mother makes a prolonged and deeply unwelcome visit from South Africa and berates her daughter for not being able to 'manage' the other servants in Mark's household, bemused as she is by Martha's ambiguous status in it. Lessing gives us an acute insight into the shifting sands of social class, and of the perpetual embarrassment of left-leaning women who, like Virginia Woolf, employed other women to do their dirty work for them. This is a theme in Francesca Wade's interesting recent sociological survey *Square Haunting*, which examines the overlapping lives of five women writers living in Bloomsbury between the wars, including Woolf.

I interviewed Lessing in 1972 for the West Coast left-of-centre glossy magazine *Ramparts*. I knew her quite well, and I remember that over lunch in my home we talked of many things – prophetic dreams, cooking, recipes, drug-taking and the new psychiatric theories of R. D. Laing. We did not talk about feminism as I knew she disliked the subject and did not like to be classified as a feminist. (For the record: she did almost all her own dirty work, all her own shopping and cooking.) She was less than gracious to the American academics who sang her praises and hailed *The Golden Notebook* as their Bible.

The Four-Gated City is just as interesting as its notorious and distinguished predecessor, though much less well known, partly, perhaps, because of its formidable length – it runs to over 700 pages of small print. She had also by this time come under the influence of the Sufi guru Idries Shah, whose spiritual views had replaced communism as a faith, and his theories are woven into the later novel. She avoided the subject of Sufism when talking to me (just as I avoided feminism when talking to her) as she sensed that I disapproved. The novel has an atmosphere of apocalyptic doom, prefigured in dreams and visions: this was the period when she was trying to persuade us all that we needed to dig nuclear bunkers, as they were doing in Switzerland. In my *Ramparts* interview, I described her as a Cassandra whom nobody would believe. She foresaw a Britain poisoned by nuclear fallout and nerve gas, looking 'like a dead mouse in a corner, injected with a deadly, glittering dew'.

This makes the novel sound unremittingly grim, and I had been reluctant to reread it, but I am so glad I did. It is prophetic, but it is also sharply observant of social reality, and parts of it are very funny. There is a good scene near the beginning where the newly arrived and penniless Martha meets Henry, a well-off contact and friend of acquaintances in South Africa, who has offered her a job: she arrives in the shabby-genteel West End restaurant before her host, is treated with 'an arrogance of bad manners' by the lean, elderly waiter, realizes she is in some subtle way incorrectly dressed, embarks on an ill-advised political discussion about poverty and the working classes with Henry and, although she has asked for pâté, is treated to 'scallop shells filled with lumps of cod covered with a cheese-coloured white sauce. That this was a restaurant where people ate, not to eat well, but to eat comfortably, she had understood from what she had seen on the plates near her . . .' Lessing goes on to catalogue the dirty tablecloth, the stale rolls, the sagging roses, the blanquette de veau which follows the coquilles, the trifle which comes under another name. 'Throughout the restaurant, people were eating nursery puddings, under French names.'

Martha notes that 'The wine, however, was very good indeed,

marvellous . . .' In short, a man's world, summed up in telling detail, a world which Martha and Lessing had come to confront.

It is interesting to note that Martha's renewed acquaintance with Henry is enabled by the fact that she had casually jotted down his telephone number on a bus ticket. Bus tickets exist no more, or not as we knew them. Mine will be the last generation to remember bus conductors and bus tickets.

One of the things that surprised me, this time round, was the amount of discussion of the merits of private versus state education. There are several references to Eton, which some of the principal characters attended, and to progressive comprehensive schooling. Education was a prominent and ideologically divisive talking point of the Sixties and Seventies and I'm not sure Lessing ever made her mind up about it. She was certainly not as committed as I was to the comprehensive system. The subject has hardly gone away, governed as we have been and are by so many Old Etonians, but it has a dated, hopeless feel to it these days. Perhaps her interest was coloured by the story of the Cambridge spies, with their public-school affiliations and their communism, and in the novel one of her many gripping sub-plots involves a character suspected of spying: her satirical portrayal of the venal journalists who pursue him is particularly acute and well informed. She was deeply interested in social class, as well as in progressive politics, and had a sharp eye for hypocrisy. She is also very good on the growing power of television (which she herself watched quite a lot):

> The television set, its back to her, emitted noises of human beings in violent conflict. This was the real educator of the children of the nation . . . they had absorbed the idea that they, 'the inheritors of our future, etc. etc.', were being fed a view of the world, life, that was all killing and violence.

As is manifested by that quotation, Lessing is not an elegant stylist. Nobody could ever praise her 'beautiful prose'. She is far too interested in getting to the truth of the matter to care much for cadence and sonority. In my *Ramparts* piece written over forty years ago I noted that:

> The point is, *The Four-Gated City* is littered with sentences that begin, bluntly, desperately, with the words 'The point is . . .' And the point follows. Most writers feel compelled to write bridging passages, to plane down the surface, to conceal their points . . . The flexibility of her writing is by now amazing: she changes tense, tone, place, she skips decades, moves from the past to the future, documents, speculates, describes, with relentless urgency. The world of *The Four-Gated City* is a different world from the world of Martha Quest, though its protagonist is the same, and has endured the same history.

I stand by that judgement and am as full of admiration as ever. I could not quite follow Lessing into the space fiction world of the *Canopus in Argus: Archives*, though I enjoyed much of her later fiction. For me *The Four-Gated City* marks a high point in her work. In it, she unites her passionate interest in people and pragmatic daily housekeeping details – the mending of drains and fixing of light switches, the cooking of meals, the washing of clothes, the coming and going of fashions and styles – with her visionary sense of the future, a future which may be even worse than she feared and we now fear.

MARGARET DRABBLE has written nineteen novels and a volume of short stories, as well as editing the *Oxford Companion to English Literature*. Her memoir, *The Pattern in the Carpet*, which revolves round the history and appeal of the jigsaw puzzle, was reissued in 2020 to mark the pandemic-inspired resurgence of interest in puzzles.

Paper Trails

CHARLES ELLIOTT

I have always been taken with the idea of treasure-hunting. Not that I have done much of it myself. I do recall searching (without success) for a reputed abandoned gold mine on Tom Ball Mountain in the New England Berkshires, and I once went so far as to put together an anthology of treasure-hunting stories, which didn't sell very well. But frankly, for me treasure-hunting is purely an intellectual sport, which is probably just as well. Reading about unexpected discoveries and adventurous expeditions is on the whole more practical than crashing through underbrush and keeping a weather eye for black bears, especially at my age.

I have to admit that the book in hand isn't ageing well either, physically. The paper is browning almost to the point of flaking and has that distinctive smell of old bookshops whose proprietors have taken in too much stock and will never again have shelf space. After all, sixty years of life as a paperback is a lot to ask of any book. I am nevertheless reluctant to put this one out of its misery to make room for some crisper and more attractive volume. *The Scholar Adventurers* (1950) still speaks to my own ancient ambitions and interests, terminated by reality equally long ago but never quite extinguished.

In case there is any confusion, I must make it plain that the treasure-hunting involved here is of a very different kind. No metal-

---

Richard Altick, *The Scholar Adventurers* (1950), is out of print but we can obtain second-hand copies.

detectors. Richard Altick's protagonists are all searching for their own versions of the Lost Ark, but unlike Indiana Jones their hunting ground is libraries, muniment rooms, family archives and other paper-choked places. Their quarry is new facts – and documents – about the lives and works of great writers.

If this sounds boring, be assured that it isn't. What we've got here is a grand collection of stories about men (and a few women) who devoted their careers to literary detection. Of course they are nearly all academics (I know, the very term is enough to put some people off), but those of us with the faintest taste for bookish adventures will quickly be caught up in their quests. Unmasking frauds, solving a 400-year-old murder, discovering long-lost manuscripts, identifying forgeries – this is the sort of thing that will be found here, and for my part I can't get enough.

Start, for example, with Altick's account of the long hunt for the papers of James Boswell, which went on for years and which, when they were finally unearthed in a cow barn in the grounds of an Irish castle, served to restore the sadly damaged reputation of the great biographer of Samuel Johnson. (The collection included an unexpected bestseller with the publication of Boswell's frank and lively *London Journal*.) Luck and monomania all played a part in the search, from the English gentleman who happened to find a cache of Boswell letters being used to wrap parcels in a shop in Boulogne in 1850 to the professors who patiently talked their way past recalcitrant Irish peers in the twentieth century. Add to that the timely involvement of a wealthy New York financier obsessed with all things Boswellian and Johnsonian, and prepared to put up the hard cash needed to bring the papers to light, and you have quite a story.

Of course, as anyone familiar with Henry James's classic document-hunting novella *The Aspern Papers* knows, the detective work required to locate the treasure is only the first part of the process. Winkling it out, or even getting a good look at it, can take years of cajoling. It is not only the heir in his collapsing British mansion, protective of his family's reputation, who can cause trouble but also collectors who, for one reason or another, see enquiring scholars as dangerous interlopers. Altick notes the feud in the Emily Dickinson family that prevented access to the reclusive poet's papers for nearly a century after her death. (They were finally sold to Harvard.) And newspaper stories about staggering prices paid for rarities at auction simply complicate matters, with 'indifference, hostility, ignorance and avarice' too often blocking the way to the researcher's goal.

Still, *The Scholar Adventurers* is devoted mainly to success, or at least something approximating it. A whole series of curious scholars spent years trying to figure out the truth about Sir Thomas Malory, author of *Le Morte d'Arthur*, one of the first books ever printed in England and the main source for tales of the King and his Round Table. To begin with, nobody knew exactly who Malory was or anything much about his life, except that at the time his book was written, he was apparently in jail. The first discovery was his identity, made by an American professor who doggedly sifted through thousands of variously spelled fifteenth-century Malorys (no computers available in 1894). But that was all. Sir Thomas Malory remained a cipher. Then in the mid-1920s came a startling development. Another researcher, working in what Altick calls 'that vast haystack of government documents' that is the Public Record Office, found a document that not only referred clearly to Malory but also described him in specific detail as an extortionist, a cattle thief, an attempted assassin and a rapist. The authorities had finally acted when he led a gang attacking a Carthusian monastery. No wonder he was in jail – or soon out of it, because he escaped.

But wait. For all the material that has been unearthed showing our author to have been a thoroughly dubious character, so far nothing incontrovertibly proves that we have the right man. And even if we do, some of the charges against him could be false, given the vastly unsettled conditions in late medieval England. So, as Altick points out, there is still more to be learned, more arguments to be settled, more work for scholars to do. Sir Thomas is not in the clear yet.

There is much less uncertainty in another of my favourite chapters. Thanks to the brilliant sleuthing of a couple of rare-book dealers, John Carter and Graham Pollard, the case of Thomas J. Wise has been settled beyond any shadow of doubt. Fraud interests and amuses me as much as treasure-hunting does, and so far as I'm concerned this case, which Altick calls 'the most sensational literary scandal of our time', has pretty much everything.

In the late nineteenth century Wise was generally regarded as the doyen of bibliographers, master of the subtlest details of priorities and points, the authority to whom everyone deferred when arguments over rare books arose. He had also assembled a magnificent library. Around 1930, however, Carter and Pollard – first working separately but then joining forces – noted some oddities about certain rare pamphlets by writers like Elizabeth Barrett Browning and John Ruskin. For one thing, there were too many of them, and for another, many had passed through the distinguished hands of Thomas J. Wise. Yet nothing was clear; in spite of their suspicions it took the two literary detectives years before the scale of the great man's culpability could be established – and even then *why* he had chosen to commit fraud remained a mystery.

We will never be without fraud in some form or other to amuse or annoy us, but the era of paper is ending. Scholars in the future probably won't find the same opportunities for exciting literary discoveries, at least in the classic treasure-hunt form. Besides, emails and computer text lack the romance of a packet of letters or a revealing diary in a forgotten attic, and they evaporate at the touch of a button. Some adjustments will have to made. In the meantime, these accounts fascinate.

CHARLES ELLIOTT is a retired editor and author of several anthologies and books of essays.

Plenty to Say

OLIVIA POTTS

A few months after my mother died, my sister and I returned home to clear out her possessions. I felt unsentimental about most of them. I readily threw away clothes, keeping only a cardigan that was the last thing she wore, and still smelled of her; I swept her extensive collection of toiletries into a large bin bag. From her jewellery, I squirrelled away only a pair of opal earrings, to wear on my wedding day.

The exception to this general rule was her book collection. Mum was a voracious reader. When I picture our birthdays, holidays, family evenings together, I always see her with a book in her hand, and I consider a love of reading my most important inheritance. So I kept as many of her books as I could, lugging them from Newcastle to London in flimsy rolling suitcases.

Among them was a complete collection of Mary Wesley's novels. I'd read Mum's copy of *The Camomile Lawn* (1984), Wesley's most famous book, as a teenager, and remembered a character called Calypso, a pair of twins, a *ménage à trois* in a London flat, and children racing along hilltops – a warm, sexy, adventurous book. When I reread it, I was amazed at all the things I'd forgotten: refugees, concentration camps, death and child abuse, all approached with an unsettling moral ambiguity.

But then, such is the nature of memory, particularly when confronted with death. Unconsciously, we twist things or repress them;

Mary Wesley, *Jumping the Queue* (1983), *The Camomile Lawn* (1984), *Harnessing Peacocks* (1985), *Not That Sort of Girl* (1987) and *A Dubious Legacy* (1992) are all available as Vintage paperbacks at £9.99 each.

we seek meaning where it may or may not lie. The book I remembered spoke of how I wanted to think about my mum. This is something that Wesley confronts often in her books, as her characters try to work each other out. In *Harnessing Peacocks* (1985), the protagonist, Hebe, says of her 12-year-old son, 'I love him but I seldom know what he is thinking.' Then there's the crushing but perceptive exchange between Jim, Hebe's love interest, and Bernard, her old friend, in the same book:

> 'It's important that I see her,' Jim insisted.
> 'Only to you.'
> Jim stared at the old man, deflated. 'I had not thought of that.'

Perhaps it is no surprise that, of all the authors my mother loved, Wesley – the author who deals in isolation, confusion, hope and all the things we don't know about those around us, whose books frequently turn on the death of a loved one – was the one I embraced after her death.

Born in 1912 in Surrey, Mary Wesley was the third child of Colonel Harold and Violet Mynors Farmer. Her childhood was tricky: her mother openly disdained her, and she went through sixteen governesses. (When she asked her mother why, the reply was simple: 'Because none of them liked you, darling.') A first marriage to Charles Swinfen Eady ended in a scandalous divorce; later, she married Eric Siepmann, whom she was with until his death in 1970. Despite her relatively wealthy upbringing, Eric's death left her destitute.

Wesley's path to publication is an astonishing one, and not simply because of her age (she was 70 when her first novel, *Jumping the Queue*, was published). She had long held writing ambitions, and had written three children's books before Siepmann's death, but she had never tackled adult fiction. Her newly strained financial position in the wake of her husband's death provided the necessary spur. She began working on a peculiar manuscript: dark and funny, genuinely tragic and life-affirming, a book of family secrets and deceit.

Jumping the Queue tells the story of Matilda, an elderly widow who has decided to end her life by taking some pills and then swimming out to sea after a picnic. She is interrupted twice, first by a gaggle of youths and then, when she has instead resolved to throw herself off a cliff, by a strange man who turns out to be a wanted killer on the run. She takes the man into her home and, subsequently, into her bed.

Mary Wesley, at the time she was struggling to write *Jumping the Queue*

Publishers weren't interested, and even her agent eventually gave up, telling Wesley that she would no longer submit the manuscript to publishers. Wesley remained resolute, and essentially began agenting her own book. Eventually, the editor James Hale expressed an interest. Wesley didn't have the money for a train fare to London to meet him; her agent had to advance her the money. When Hale had read the whole thing, Wesley asked him what he would like to change. He replied, 'Not a word.' *Jumping the Queue* was published in 1983 and received an overwhelming critical and commercial reception. Over the next fourteen years Wesley went on to write another nine books, which sold a total of 3 million copies.

Her third book, *Harnessing Peacocks* (1985), is the one that has my heart. It tells the story of Hebe – like me, a cook – whose family, on discovering she is pregnant, plan an abortion for her. Instead, Hebe runs away, and we meet her in London, where she is now living with her 12-year-old son Silas, whom she supports through a combination of cooking (for elderly, rich women who live alone) and sex work (for their sons and sons-in-law). The themes that recur in Wesley's writing are alive and well in *Harnessing Peacocks*: complicated relationships within families, rejection of class, sex, and the fundamental unknowability of other people, even – sometimes particularly – those who are closest to us, or bound to us by blood. Hebe's rejection of social mores and conventional morality is what brings her her son, her friendships and the unconventional life that she loves. When she encounters her cruel grandparents in the modern day (they do not recognize her) she realizes the change she has engendered in herself: 'It seemed so very long ago, yet nothing about them had changed. Except, thought Hebe in joyous surprise, catching sight in the driving mirror of the striped bag on the back seat, except that I am no longer afraid.'

Wesley is remembered for her frank and enthusiastic treatment of sex, although she maintained that the reaction was overblown. As she put it,

> People are startled by my books because they think, how can an old woman write about sex? As though one forgets it, as though it isn't in everything you see, breathe, watch – because sex is so enjoyable and so funny – how could one forget it? The idea that people go on being sexy all their life is little explored in fiction. What do people think 'happy ever after' means? It goes on and on; it doesn't end.

Her incredulity seems disingenuous to me. Because Wesley's sex isn't just sex – it's polyamory, and sex work, and many other things besides. Wesley's women are sexual instigators and pleasure-seekers; virgins and old ladies. Above all, what dominates is funny, liberated enjoyment of sex. This sexual diversity is seldom found in any fiction of the time, much less that written by female authors of Wesley's generation and class.

And, of course, it extrapolates outwards: the sex that these women engage in is a mark of their unashamed appetites – not just in sex, but in food, in life. ('I am a very expensive cook,' Hebe declares. 'The same applies to bed.') Calypso, the main character in *The Camomile Lawn* who recurs in many of Wesley's other novels, remarks to her nephew in *Harnessing Peacocks*, 'Be bold about it, don't let them put you off, do what you want in life.' It feels like a credo. In interviews Wesley always ducked the point, simply bemoaning the fact that the young think they 'invented sex'. I think she did herself a disservice. In her books, women of all ages take charge of their own destiny, for good and for bad. For me, and perhaps for my mum, that felt radical, and important.

Throughout her writing life, Wesley denied autobiographical influences on her writing. But to the reader they seem palpable. *Jumping the Queue* was written shortly after the death of her own husband, albeit one more beloved than her protagonist's, and focuses on Matilda's suicide. Wesley herself seems to have sunk into a deep depression after her husband's death; she wrote 'Do not resuscitate' on the front of her diary, and only removed the instruction after landing her book deals. Her first experience of sex, as told to Patrick Marnham, her biographer, closely mirrors Rose Peel's loss of her virginity in *Not That Sort of Girl* (1987), and the cold, cruel grandparents in *Harnessing Peacocks* bear many similarities to her own parents. More generally, the lives of Wesley's protagonists seem to echo Wesley's own life as they move away from wealthy, repressed upbringings or wealthy, unsatisfying first marriages towards a life directed by their own desires or happiness.

Hale remained Wesley's editor for the whole of her writing life and said that she was 'the first serious writer to be sold as though she were Catherine Cookson in a full-blooded commercial way'. Of course, when literary people use the word 'commercial' it often isn't a compliment. Anita Brookner, reviewing *A Dubious Legacy* for the *Spectator* in 1992, dismissed Wesley's writing as 'stereotyped, nostalgic, reassuring, romantic, tasteful, well-bred, very slight, very unreal and very tedious'. But Wesley's writing strikes me as the exact opposite of reassuring or tasteful, and it is explicitly critical of the nostalgic, the romantic or the well-bred. The sex is fun but rarely romantic, and her books are packed with domestic violence, murder, suicide and incest.

What I – and I suspect many others – admire is that despite all this, the darkness doesn't dominate. Wesley's books are leavened with a sparkling wit, and their pace speaks of a woman who has found her voice late in life, and who has a whole host of books inside her.

Asked why she stopped writing fiction at the age of 84, Wesley replied, 'If you haven't got anything to say, don't say it.' Again, I suspect she was being glib. But perhaps that's just because I don't want it to be true. I want to live in the world of Mary Wesley's books, where women always, always have more to say, and more often than not also have the chance to say it.

Mary Wesley died on 30 December 2002, aged 90. Among her many other accomplishments, she taught me to see my mother as a woman as well as my mother – a woman with things to say, and with a complex life that will remain unknown and unknowable to me – and that, amidst the darkness that life can bring, there is always a place for humour, for pleasure, for self-direction.

OLIVIA POTTS is a writer and chef. Her first book, *A Half-Baked Idea: How grief, love and cake took me from the courtroom to Le Cordon Bleu*, is published by Fig Tree.

Gone Fishing

ADAM SISMAN

For me, some books act like a time machine, leading me back into my past, reminding me of how it felt to be young. This doesn't happen often, but when it does, the effect is intense. Sensations that I had forgotten arise afresh, and the world seems new again.

Hugh Falkus's *The Stolen Years* (1965) is one of those books, evoking for me the simplicity and innocence of boyhood. Not that his upbringing was anything like mine: far from it. He was a child of the inter-war period, inhabiting first a converted Thames barge on the Essex coast, and later an old sixty-ton, straight-stemmed cutter, moored in a Devon estuary; I grew up in the 1960s and 1970s, in a house in West London. Nevertheless, his reminiscences stir my own.

Falkus's childhood was spent among mudflats, reed-beds and shorelines. He caught his first fish at the age of 4, learned to shoot when he was 6, and became an expert helmsman while still in short trousers. He passed many contented hours afloat, messing about in boats, sometimes with an adult, sometimes alone. Most of these boats had rotting boards, unreliable engines or ancient sails, liable to tear in a strong wind; heading out to sea in one of these was always a risk. What is especially striking to the modern reader is the freedom the young Falkus was allowed to roam unaccompanied, on land or water. No fuss then about handing a shotgun to a boy and letting him venture out on the marshes before dawn in pursuit of wildfowl.

The Stolen Years is a memoir of this happy time. There is no contin-

---

Hugh Falkus, *The Stolen Years* (1965), is out of print but we can obtain second-hand copies.

uous narrative; each chapter forms a separate episode, and by the end of the book the small boy met at the outset has become a young man. An early chapter extols the qualities of Sally, in the same class as Hugh at infant school, who for a modest consideration would lift her skirts and 'show you my bum'; the penultimate chapter is an elegy to a dark, slim girl in a green dress, glimpsed standing in the lamplight in the doorway of a Devon farmhouse, never to be seen again.

These two chapters are the exception, however; otherwise women scarcely feature in the book. Neither does school; most of the action takes place outside, in or around water. Incidents that might seem inconsequential to an adult are related with a child-like zeal that imbues them with emotional significance. Thus we are told of an epic struggle with a giant eel, dragged to the surface, that thrashes its monstrous tail before plunging back into the depths, leaving a line broken and a rod smashed; of a huge lobster, speared in a rock-pool, and triumph turning to despair when the captive crustacean, after feigning lifelessness, stealthily escapes back into its element.

One of the most dramatic chapters describes sailing single-handed into a gale as the sea whips up into a fury and the light fades, the old yacht plunging into the blackness, taking on water as its worn-out seams gape under the strain. Falkus manages to navigate a foaming reef and reach the shelter of the estuary, but his boat is sinking beneath him. Eventually he beaches her and falls asleep in the bows, exhausted. Soon after sunrise he wakes, cold and stiff, the taste of salt on his lips, and jumps down on to firm sand, his legs rubbery. Sadly he contemplates his beloved old boat, knowing that she will never sail again.

These stories are told in lucid, muscular prose. In Falkus's vivid descriptions one can smell the tang of the sea, feel the cold wind against the skin and the cling of wet clothes in driving rain, hear the crunch of boots on frozen ground. Through the clear gaze of a child we also meet old eccentrics such as Puggy Dimmond, a one-eyed old man with a long, bent nose who lives alone aboard an ancient fishing smack, retired to the mud of an Essex estuary.

There is comedy as well as drama in these anecdotes, much of it deriving from the mistaken optimism of Falkus's sweet-natured father. One relates an evening sail across the Channel to Holland, aboard a converted ship's lifeboat. Tacking against a headwind for hour after hour, they lose their way in thickening fog and decide to anchor until morning. When the day dawns and the mist clears, they find themselves back where they had started.

The book opens with a character sketch of Falkus's father:

It is true that my father had other interests besides fishing. Boats and budgerigars, for instance, and occasionally the world of commerce. But fishing was the thread which bound his life together and he fished, as he lived, with infectious and inexhaustible enthusiasm. A great big broad fellow, with a merry mouth and an astonishing constitution, he lived to the fullness of eighty-five, and to say that there were not many like him is no sentimental exaggeration. There have been men who fished longer; many who fished more skilfully; but few, I fancy, who fished harder . . .

During the contemplation of a fishing trip his naturally sanguine temperament reached a state of sustained euphoria bordering on the beatific. Lunatic, my mother called it.

The final chapter tells of a wild December night when Falkus's father, who had been fishing that afternoon from a dinghy on a reef where the tide ran fast, fails to come home. Seized with apprehension, Falkus runs down to the shore. The wind is blowing in great gusts, with flurries of snow; the weed-covered rocks are wet and slimy. Peering into the blackness, he makes out something rolling in a ridge of foam – his father's dinghy, still anchored but capsized. The man himself is nowhere to be seen. By this time, Falkus calculates, six hours must have passed since he went overboard. Frantically he tries to imagine what his father might have done: by kicking off his boots and outer clothes, he might have been able to stay afloat for a while. The current would have carried him towards the *Susannah*, an old fishing smack moored three-quarters of a mile away, just off the main channel. It is just possible that he found it in the failing light and managed to climb aboard.

Flashing his torch, Falkus runs panting towards a small cluster of rowing boats drawn up on the sand. Miraculously he finds one still equipped with rowlocks and oars – though not a pair. He pushes off into the night, and with the strength of desperation rows across the choppy water, trying to guess where *Susannah* lies. Then he hears a voice crying out; and immediately afterwards, a shadowy hull looms out of the darkness. Falkus swings the rowing boat into the lee of the smack, grasps the gunwale and peers over the side. There is his father, crouching in the cockpit, clad only in his underwear. 'Oh Hugh,' he says, 'I am glad to see you.'

The adult Falkus was a handsome, virile man, with a commanding presence. After leaving school he learned to fly and enrolled in the RAF. In the summer of 1940, his Spitfire was shot down over France after he had downed three enemy bombers; underneath his flying suit he was still wearing his pyjamas. The Germans took him for a spy and sentenced him to death. In a gesture of contempt he turned his back on the firing squad to watch trout rising in a river outside the fence – before receiving a miraculous, last-minute reprieve. As a prisoner-of-war, he spent years tunnelling in a series of frustrated attempts to escape, until he eventually succeeded, reaching England only ten days before the German surrender.

After the war Falkus became known as a broadcaster on natural history and made a series of award-winning films. It was while he was shooting one of these, about basking sharks, that his boat was caught in a sudden squall off the west coast of Ireland and sank. Falkus took charge and, as the strongest swimmer, struck out for the shore, leaving his wife and the three members of the film crew clinging to floating debris. After a long struggle he made landfall and raised the alarm, but by the time help arrived, the others had perished.

In the final paragraphs of *The Stolen Years* Falkus reflects on his father, and on a life well lived.

I like to think that he found his lonely creek – and lies always by the sea-lavender-covered marshlands, where there is no sound but the distant sea and the curlews crying.

In later years, my own narrow escapes and a world crashed into ruin put me beyond wonder at the mystery of life on this spinning planet. We cling by our fingernails to the rim of a great wheel, and some of us give up and slip off, and some cling for a time, and some stick. Although sooner or later all visions fade; the most tenacious grip loosens.

What do men do with stolen time? Everyone lives in the tight little house of his mind, each with its own façade, and no one really knows what goes on in the next house. But sometimes, when the wind raved in the chimney, we would sit together snug beside a fire in some smoke-darkened tap-room and drink a pint to the stolen years.

Falkus wrote several other books, among them one revered as the bible of sea-trout fishing, yet he considered *The Stolen Years* his best. Some years after his death a 'warts-and-all' biography by Chris Newton, *Hugh Falkus: A Life on the Edge*, revealed an unpleasant side to his character. In later life, it seems, Falkus became an irascible bully and a sexual predator. It is perhaps better not to know too much about one's heroes.

Yet nothing can spoil the pleasure I find in rereading *The Stolen Years*. I have only to dip into Falkus's memoir of his boyhood and I am 11 years old again, my hand poised over a split-cane fishing rod or gripping an oak tiller.

ADAM SISMAN is a writer, specializing in biography. His most recent book is *The Professor and the Parson: A Story of Desire, Deceit and Defrocking* (2019).

Magical Talisman

SUE GAISFORD

It's silly to covet a piece of jewellery. When would you really wear Marie-Antoinette's necklace or the Hope Diamond? Even the glittering parures paraded by red-carpet celebrities are borrowed, insured for millions and necessitate the accompaniment of burly heavies all the way back to the soft obscurity of velvet and safe. Ridiculous. But – all the same – how lovely it would be, just once, for a few minutes, to hold in one's hands the ring of the Aquilas.

A ring is the story that has no end, a magical talisman. For the likes of Wagner or Tolkien it's nothing but trouble, but for Rosemary Sutcliff it is benign, even life-affirming. Hers is a heavy gold man's ring, its bezel set with a flawed emerald into which is carved a dolphin. Fashioned long ago in Rome, it is already slightly battered when, in *The Eagle of the Ninth*, it is handed back to young Marcus Flavius Aquila by a tribal warlord who had taken it from his murdered father. Over the succeeding centuries and another six magnificent novels it is stolen, returned, lost, clumsily enlarged, rediscovered and proudly worn by generations of his descendants. And all the while his bloodline is renewed and enriched, throughout the great waves of invasion, resistance, settlement, intermarriage and miscegenation that followed the departure of the Legions.

The series that began in the Sussex downland has, by the last two books, moved to the north-west coast of England and the Hebridean islands, where the Vikings are expanding their empire. In *Sword Song* (published posthumously, in 1997) our hero Bjorn Sigurdson is a young Norwegian with a lot to learn. No sooner has he arrived at Rafnglas, where his brother has settled, than he drowns a man who

had kicked his dog. He hadn't meant to
drown him, and he'd had no idea that the
man was a Christian monk, but five years
of banishment is his fate and he sails away
to the big bad Viking city of Dublin,
where ale-houses are as thick on the ground as
autumn leaves, and where he is comprehensively
mugged.

C. Walter Hodges

Now his adventures really begin, working
on the speedy and nimble longships,
pillaging a bit, feasting, trading, raiding
and surviving spectacular storms, learning
all the while from his elders who, even in
the most impenetrable fogs, can navigate
'by wave-patterns and the sight and
sound of the sea', and who know the
secrets of deep water through their
eyes and ears and the soles of their
feet. But it is only when he is shipwrecked off the Welsh coast and
encounters the beautiful, beleaguered Angharad that he really grows
up. She retrieves from a silken string around her neck a glinting green
ring and, with a shock, we recognize her as the descendant of the
young Roman soldier who once sought his lost father, so many
centuries earlier.

Two hundred years and several generations on, those seafaring
days are just the stuff of legend for Bjorn and Angharad's descendant.
Bjorni, or Little Bear, lives in the household of the semi-mythical Jarl
Buthar above Buttermere, the lake which still bears his name. The
Jarl's figurehead, hung high in the smoky rafters of his Hearth Hall,
is all that physically remains of the longships, though their stories live
on in the music of the harpers, and still, *in extremis*, they call on the
old gods, on Thor and on Odin. It is twenty years after the Battle of
Hastings, but the Normans have still not conquered the mountain

fastness of Cumberland, nor have they written of it in their *Domesday Book*, for the last of the unassimilated Vikings have always held out against their frequent attacks. This ongoing defence of their stronghold, their traditions and their way of life is the background to *The Shield Ring* (1956).

The Vikings have left little mark on the British landscape (though more underneath it) but their language survives – in the days of the week, of course, and in the hard Norse syllables describing Lakeland: fell, force, beck and thwaite; ness and kirk, rill and rigg; tarn, thorp, dale and skull. And from their sagas and oral traditions come many of the most thrilling, shattering passages in these last two books. As always, the stories are rooted in fact. The mighty Helm Wind, for example, the only named wind in these islands, is as respected for its lethal strength today as when, in *The Shield Ring*, it sweeps suddenly over Cross Fell, mowing down the Norman cavalry by its immense force as overwhelmingly as Pharaoh's armies had once been swallowed by the Red Sea.

In the final chapter the Jarl's son, Aikin the Beloved, has died in the last great battle. Now he lies in the Hearth Hall, where the guttering torchlight plays 'on the smoke-dimmed shields that hung from the house-beam . . . bringing the snarling mask of the ancient figurehead leaping forward out of obscurity; then sinking so that all the hall was lost again save for the flame-lit ring of warriors about their leader's body'. The next day, he is carried up to his 'howe-laying' in the place still known as Aiken's Knoll, on the fells above Keskadale, 'And his sword-brothers piled the stones high, and left him to the wind and the rain and the curlews calling.'

And, at the very end, Bjorni leaves the settlement, along with the Saxon orphan Frytha who has lived and fought alongside him, dressed his war wounds and saved his life. They make for his forefathers' settlement high up in Eskdale, just below the already ancient Roman fort at Hardknott on the slopes of Scafell. To leave them there, among the little Herdwick sheep, with the emerald ring and a harp and a jewelled dagger whose histories we know well – better than they do themselves – is to experience that poignant sense of bereavement that only the very finest fiction can evoke.

SUE GAISFORD has spent some time in the Dark Ages recently and finds them marginally preferable to the twenty-first century.

Slightly Foxed has reissued all seven of Rosemary Sutcliff's Roman and post-Roman novels as a set in a limited and numbered cloth-bound edition of 2,000 copies.

The final two books in the series, *Sword Song* (228pp) and *The Shield Ring* (216pp), are now available (subscribers per copy for each title: UK & Eire £17, Overseas £19; non-subscribers: UK & Eire £19, Overseas £21). All prices include post and packing. Copies may be ordered by post (53 Hoxton Square, London N1 6PB), by phone (020 7033 0258) or via our website www.foxedquarterly.com.

The first five books in the series, *The Eagle of the Ninth*, *The Silver Branch*, *Frontier Wolf*, *The Lantern Bearers* and *Dawn Wind*, are also still available.

The Ubiquitous Canadian

MICHAEL BARBER

Charles Ritchie (1906–95) was a witty, cultivated Canadian diplomat whose voluminous diaries, a blend of anecdote, commentary and confession, were an 'escape hatch' from the confines of his profession. Much of what he wrote was too candid to be published. For instance in 1962, when stationed in Washington, he met Harold Macmillan, who was trying to ingratiate himself with President Kennedy. Macmillan, he waspishly noted, 'drips "manner" like a buttered crumpet'. This must have been the occasion on which Kennedy disconcerted Macmillan, a complaisant husband, by revealing that he got a 'terrible headache' if he didn't have a woman every two or three days. Unlike Macmillan, Ritchie would have understood. In January 1941, having kissed goodbye to his current squeeze, a pretty young ballerina who was off on tour, he looked forward to 'early and varied infidelities during her absence'.

From a well-connected Nova Scotian family, Ritchie was educated at Harvard, the Sorbonne and Oxford, where he was unusual in having a mistress. I learnt this when writing the life of Anthony Powell, who overlapped with Ritchie at Oxford, though I don't think they ever met. Unlike most of the 'Brideshead Generation', Powell was unimpressed by Oxford, not least because girls were off limits. He thought undergraduates then were 'retarded adolescents', a verdict endorsed by this passage from *An Appetite for Life* (1977), Ritchie's undergraduate diaries, which I came across in the course of my

Charles Ritchie, *The Siren Years: A Canadian Diplomat Abroad, 1937–1945* (1974), is out of print but we can obtain second-hand copies.

research into Powell: 'These English undergraduates do seem incredibly young . . . They are mostly virgins though they would rather die than admit it . . . They talk about sex a lot but it is mainly smut and endless limericks.'

Angular, beak-nosed, narrow-chested and bespectacled, Ritchie did not fit the mould of a philanderer, but as is apparent from *The Siren Years* (1974), an edited version of the war diary he kept, he had little difficulty in realizing his 'impure thoughts'. You get the feeling that as well as getting off with women, he also got on with them – and they reciprocated.

Ritchie arrived at Canada House in London in January 1939, by which time it was becoming apparent that Munich was not a reprieve but a stay of execution. As Private Secretary to the High Commissioner, Vincent Massey, he had to tread carefully because there was no guarantee that Canada, under its isolationist premier Mackenzie King, would join Britain in another European war. Nor did Ritchie find much enthusiasm for war in the elevated social circles he frequented: 'I cannot believe', he wrote in May 1939, 'that this country will go to war for the Polish corridor.' But go to war it did, becoming, overnight, a garrison state. On 8 September Ritchie woke at 3 a.m. to the sound of sirens and asked himself, 'Was there a time when we did not all carry gas masks?'

For almost a year the sirens sounded in vain. Then at the end of August 1940 the London Blitz began. Though nothing like as apocalyptic as people had feared, it turned the Home Front into the front line. The West End took a pasting. Returning home one morning after a night out of town Ritchie found his flat in Arlington Street, just behind the Ritz, reduced to a heap of dirty rubble, with bits of his bespoke suits, 'wet and blackened', visible among the bricks. As well as his suits, the cost of which he doubted he could reclaim in full, he particularly regretted the loss of his little green commonplace book.

After a brief sojourn at the Dorchester – 'a fortress propped up with money bags', into which 'the sweepings of the Riviera have been

washed up' – Ritchie then spent a few weeks at Brooks's, one of several clubs to which he belonged. Clubland was a rich source of
anecdote. At the dining table of Pratt's, where it was not done to
pull rank, he saw Anthony Eden, then Foreign Secretary, discomfited
by a subaltern. Eden had been 'holding forth at length on the
Mediterranean situation'. The subaltern, just back from the Middle
East, 'turned to a friend and said, "I do not know who that man is
but he is talking awful balls." Immense satisfaction of all members.'

On another occasion Ritchie was told that Stalin was bored stiff
by the British Ambassador, Stafford Cripps, because he would drone
on about Communism when all Stalin wanted to hear about was
Edward VIII and Mrs Simpson. 'He could not understand why Mrs
Simpson was not liquidated.' (Years later, when serving as Canadian
Ambassador to the UN, Ritchie met the Duchess of Windsor at a
party, looking 'ravaged but unsated . . . engagingly full of curiosity
and with a nose tilted for scandal').

The black-out, and the 'fumbling' it begat, was something that
Ritchie, like everyone else, learned to live with. In town you 'fumbled
for your front door key' while bits of shrapnel drifted down 'almost
like snowflakes'. Country-house weekends, a welcome change from
the oppression of a London Sunday, posed a different sort of challenge after dark. So scrupulously did your hosts enforce the black-out
that at night you found yourself 'fumbling your way by the light of
a small hand torch along black corridors filled with unfamiliar furni-
ture to the WC (which one had failed to mark by daylight) or
alternatively to the bedroom of your girlfriend'.

On one weekend away Ritchie met Nancy Mitford, 'a queer mix-
ture of county and sophistication', who inspired him to try and
convey the essence of the milieu to which he thought she belonged,
that of Evelyn Waugh's novels:

In love as in conversation a flavour of insolence is appreciated.
With both sexes the thing admired is to do what you want just

as long as you want to and not a moment longer. Hence the speed with which partners change in this game, which requires a good eye, a cool nerve and a capacity to take punishment as in any other kind of sport. Toughness is the favourite virtue. Any form of cry-babyishness is taboo except among pansies, in whom it is recognized as an innate characteristic which does not affect their essential toughness . . . Discretion is looked upon as a paltry virtue like thrift. Their gossip is so frank, so abundant and so detailed it is a wonder that their lives are not even more complicated than they are.

One of Ritchie's early jobs at the High Commission was arranging safe passage to Canada for rich people's offspring. He sensed that the Old Gang was on the run, and despite his appetite for 'worldly glitter and bustle' saw social change as a welcome consequence of total war. He predicted, correctly, that most Englishmen now had 'no use for the Empire which they consider an embarrassment and a bore'. His boss said his dispatches 'read like socialist speeches'.

Until Germany invaded Russia – 'an act of madness on Hitler's part' – Ritchie feared that the Nazis would never be defeated and that the best that could be hoped for was a stalemate. After Pearl Harbor he saw light at the end of the tunnel, while recording 'the very human sardonic satisfaction' that greeted the attack. So far as many British were concerned, the Yanks had it coming to them, and their indignation at 'treachery' fell on deaf ears: 'It is like a hardened old tart who hears a girl crying because a man has deceived her for the first time.'

In his Foreword Ritchie apologizes for the 'disconnected' nature of the diary: 'Situations are left up in the air. Questions are not answered. All one can say is that this is what that life was like.' One question he does answer, albeit somewhat obliquely, is the identity of this woman: 'When I die they will find some woman's name written on my heart – I do not know myself who it will be!' Ritchie wrote that after admitting that he was now smitten with the ballerina: 'She is my perennial type.' But it was not the ballerina who would steal his heart. Within a few months of meeting the novelist Elizabeth Bowen in February 1941 he had become her lover. Less than a year later he confessed that 'this attachment is nothing transient but will bind me as long as I live'.

So what did this philanderer see in a married woman who was seven years older than him and not, by conventional standards, a beauty? Both Victoria Glendinning, in her edition of Bowen's letters and diaries, and Lara Feigel in *The Love-Charm of Bombs* have given detailed accounts of what passed between Ritchie and Bowen over the next thirty-two years, relying considerably on Ritchie's original diaries, only about a tenth of which were published. Without being lewd, Ritchie is frank about the physical attraction he immediately felt for Bowen, musing soon after they first slept together, 'How can a woman of forty with gold bangles and the face of a woman of forty and the air of a don's wife, how can such a woman have such a body – like Donatello's *David* I told her when I first saw what it was like. Those small firm breasts, that modelled neck set with such beauty on her shoulders, that magnificent back . . .'

Readers of *The Siren Years*, published a year after Bowen's death in 1973, are denied such carnal reflections. And with good reason. In 1948, realizing that it would be a good career move, Ritchie married his cousin Sylvia Smellie. It was not a love match, but it was a very successful partnership that would help propel him to the top of the diplomatic ladder. Sylvia must have known about his feelings for Bowen, otherwise, as we learn from Ritchie's Epilogue, she would not have endorsed 'the publication of this book'. But presumably she drew the line at his opening the bedroom door.

Ritchie himself also drew the line at discussing 'official business', thus running the risk, as he admitted, of being seen as a privileged loafer. At times, it is true, you do feel that like 'the Loot' in Waugh's *Unconditional Surrender*, for Ritchie 'there was no corner of the social world where he was not familiar'. A favourite haunt of his was the 400 Club, a raffish joint popular with Guards officers and their girls. He was there when the Café de Paris, just opposite, was hit, and overheard a girl say to her guardsman escort, 'Darling, it was *rather* awful when they brought out all those *black* men' – a reference to 'Snake-Hips' Johnson and his band, most of whom were killed.

In January 1945 Ritchie was posted back to Ottawa, and in April he attended the San Francisco Conference which drew up the United Nations Charter. After so long spent in a city under siege, where even the sun appeared to be rationed, he found San Francisco magical: 'The sun shines perpetually, the streets are thronged, there are American sailors everywhere with their girls and this somehow adds to the musical comedy atmosphere. You expect them at any moment to break into song and dance, and the illusion is heightened because every shop and café wafts light music from thousands of radios.'

Only the Soviet delegation under Molotov, flanked by 'husky gorillas from the NKVD', cast a chill. How to combat this chill, without responding in kind, would preoccupy Ritchie for the rest of his diplomatic career. But as is apparent from his subsequent diaries – *Diplomatic Passport* (1981) and *Storm Signals* (1983) – he never lost his appetite for life.

MICHAEL BARBER was born in London during 'the siren years'. Try as he might, he can't remember the war at all.

A Smooth Man in a Trilby

CLARISSA BURDEN

I was 13 and mad about horses when I was presented with *Brat Farrar*. The name of its author, Josephine Tey, meant nothing to me at the time and the title didn't tell me much either, but it had a picture of a horse on the cover, and that was enough for me. It proved to be the story of an imposture in which the reader knows more than the characters. I read it then and loved it, and I still do. Some years later, browsing through a box of second-hand books outside a small antique shop, I came across another of Tey's books and, remembering the first, went in and bought it. It cost 10p. Thus began a lifelong devotion.

Josephine Tey was a Scot, born Elizabeth Mackintosh in Inverness in 1896. She graduated from a physical training college near Birmingham and worked in various schools, and as a VAD nurse during the Great War. By 1923, her mother was dying, so she returned to Inverness and then stayed on to care for her father. Here, she began a new career, writing poems, short stories and plays. Always anxious to maintain her privacy, she adopted the pen-name of Gordon Daviot, a name by which some readers, including even her *Times* obituarist, knew her ever after.

Her first and most successful play was

Josephine Tey's Inspector Grant novels – *The Man in the Queue* (1929), *A Shilling for Candles* (1936), *The Franchise Affair* (1948), *To Love and Be Wise* (1950), *The Daughter of Time* (1951) and *The Singing Sands* (1952) – are all available as Arrow paperbacks at £8.99 each.

Richard of Bordeaux which opened in the West End in 1932 starring John Gielgud, who became a lifelong friend. Subsequent plays did less well, and perhaps it was this that made her concentrate on fiction. Now writing as Josephine Tey (taken from her mother's Christian name and her English grandmother's surname), she wrote eleven novels, mostly detective stories, between 1929 and 1952. They were an instant success and several were made into films. She died of liver cancer at the age of 55, and her last novel, *The Singing Sands* (1952), was published posthumously.

My 10p book was *The Man in the Queue* (1929), the first to feature Inspector Alan Grant of Scotland Yard. A recurrent sleuth has always been a favoured device for thriller-writers: Agatha Christie had her Hercule Poirot, Dorothy L. Sayers her Lord Peter Wimsey. However, in my opinion no one has ever invented a detective to equal the style and charm of Inspector Alan Grant.

We are not told much about Grant to begin with, but there are enough hints in the various books to put together a portrait. He lives in a flat in Wigmore Street with a housekeeper who looks after him, and he drives a respectable car, a lifestyle he can maintain due to a fortunate legacy from an aunt. He is a man of the world, fond of good dinners and knowledgeable about wine, and he often escorts Marta Hallard, the glamorous and talented actress who appears in many of the books: 'If he was useful to Marta as a cavalier when she needed one, she was even more useful to him as a window on the world . . . Marta was Grant's "leper's squint" on the theatre.' Of course, Tey knew a great deal about London theatre from her days as a playwright and frequently brought that knowledge into her novels.

Although Grant was supposedly born in a Midlands town, like his creator he has Scottish blood and takes every excuse to get up to the Highlands and go fishing. This love of fishing is a useful device. Once she has got him to Scotland, Tey can write freely about the rivers, moors and hills which she obviously loved deeply, but she also uses the ploy as part of Grant's detective work. He can spend a day on the river, rod in hand, apparently enjoying his sport even if he catches no fish, and it provides him with the perfect cover for observing his suspect.

The Man in the Queue was a success, and the character of this new detective must surely have had something to do with it. The plot revolves around an inconspicuous man near the front of a long queue for the last performance of a popular musical. As the doors of the theatre open and the queue shuffles eagerly forward, the man slumps to the ground. 'And rising slantwise from the grey tweed of his coat was a little silver thing that winked wickedly in the baleful light. It was the handle of a dagger.'

It is Grant of the Yard who is called in to solve the mystery. He swings into action, helped by his sidekick Sergeant Williams who is large and pink and who, to his chagrin, looks like everyone's idea of a policeman. Together they scour London, but the man they want eludes them and flees to the Highlands. An arrest is made and the wanted man is brought back to London to stand trial. But Grant is worried. He has the uncomfortable feeling that he has got the wrong man. Unlike some other fictional detectives, Grant has the humility to believe he can be mistaken. Eventually, and I don't want to give away the ending, he lights on the true murderer. As, indeed, he always will.

In Tey's second book featuring Grant, *A Shilling for Candles* (1936), his role broadens. The body of a young woman, who turns out to be a well-known singer and actress, is discovered on a lonely beach. Grant alone is sure that this is not suicide. He pursues his instinct against the advice of his chief and, collecting around him an eclectic group of helpers and suspects, he triumphs at the end of an intricate plot. In her third book, *The Franchise Affair* (1948), Grant plays only a small part. In this strange case, a mother and daughter who live in a large isolated house called The Franchise are accused of abducting a young girl, keeping her locked up and forcing her to work for them. The local solicitor, asked for help, becomes fascinated by the women and it is he who follows up clues and eventually finds the answer. Grant remains in the background, available for advice, but making only one visit to The Franchise.

Probably the best-known of all Tey's detective novels is *The Daughter of Time* (1951, see *SF* no. 8) in which a bedridden Grant amuses himself by trying to solve a historical mystery, that of the murder of the Princes in the Tower. This is a brilliant device. Grant can ruminate on a postcard-sized reproduction of the portrait of Richard III (now in the National Gallery) while a young assistant with access to the British Museum Reading Room does the research, consulting many books on the fifteenth century and rudely dismissing Thomas More's definitive account as mere hearsay. Despite all the action being confined to Grant's hospital room, the reader is taken through Richard's reign at an energetic canter. The conclusion, that Henry VII was certainly the killer of the two boys and Richard III an innocent who has been vilified by history, may not please everyone, but it satisfied Grant and makes for a very good story. Indeed, in 1990 the book was chosen by the British Crime Writers' Association as the greatest mystery novel of all time.

Fishing clothes aside, when in London Alan Grant is always well turned out. In some later editions, the illustrator Mark Smith represents him as dressed in a suit with a tie, well-polished shoes, sometimes a classic belted mackintosh, always a brown trilby: pleasingly, this is exactly as I had imagined him.

> If Grant had an asset beyond the usual ones of devotion to duty and a good supply of brains and courage . . . the last thing he looked like was a police officer. He was of medium height and slight in build, and he was – now, if I say dapper, of course you will immediately think of something like a tailor's dummy, something perfected out of all individuality, and Grant is most certainly not that.

He is also popular. So why has this delightful man never married? Although not particularly sociable, he is highly eligible. Occasionally his thoughts do run on marriage, for example with Marta Hallard or with Zoe, Lady Kintallen, an attractive widow who is also passionate about fishing. Perhaps Josephine Tey was a little in love with her charming creation and wanted to keep him to herself. Or perhaps there is some slight ambiguity about him. In the last Grant novel, *The Singing Sands*, he is travelling to the Highlands, on the advice of a psychologist, after suffering from a breakdown during which he has been prey to claustrophobia and panic attacks. He is half-ashamed of admitting to such weakness, but a quiet time of recuperation at the home of his cousin Laura is needed. He also intends to do some fishing. Given the times, could this be a clue to something that could not be spoken of or written about openly?

It is now nearly seventy years since Inspector Alan Grant made his last appearance. It is interesting to speculate on how a twenty-first-century Grant might have matured, had his creator lived longer. He would have kept his smooth London image – no James Bond derring-do for him. He would still appreciate good living. And he would undoubtedly still stand for good against evil.

Tey's elegant, pellucid prose is always a joy to read, although aspects of her books now seem, inevitably, a little dated and mannered, and a modern reader will wince at some of the distinctly un-pc views expressed. Still, she succeeds magnificently in transporting the reader back to her own period, the 1930s and '40s, a time when all men wore hats when out of doors, when it was possible to drive through London without ever encountering a traffic jam, and when Scotland Yard always got its man.

CLARISSA BURDEN lives in a small village in Kent. She reviews books, has edited a poetry anthology, and is on the judging panel for the annual Authors' Club Best First Novel Award. This involves exhaustive reading of novels, some good, some bad and lots indifferent.

Dreaming of Cheese

JOHN SMART

When I was writing a biography of John Hayward, T. S. Eliot's flat-sharer and friend for many years, I was intrigued to come across a letter from Eliot to *The Times*. It was a reply to a certain Sir John Squire who wanted to erect a statue to the creator of Stilton cheese. Who was Squire and why was this distinguished man of letters bothered about cheese? It was time to look at Squire's original letter in the British Library.

The story really began with another letter to *The Times*. In 1935 M. Theodore Rousseau, a Frenchman visiting London, complained that he could not get Stilton at any London restaurant. He bemoaned the lack of interest the English took in their native cheese. If France had invented something as delicious, he wrote, he was sure that a statue would have been erected – as had been the case with Madame Harel, the creator of Camembert. A brisk correspondence followed. Some writers had managed to find Stilton; others were told it was out of season or faced blank incomprehension. One correspondent noted that so-called Cheshire cheese was an outrage to those who knew the real thing and that even good restaurants only offered diners a choice between 'pink' and 'yellow' cheese.

As a habitual letter-writer to *The Times*, Sir John Squire, poet, editor of the monthly *London Mercury* and man-about-town, pounced on the complaint. He extolled the merits of British cheese and asked: 'What is killing the native cheese industry?' Perhaps, he

John Squire (ed.), *Cheddar Gorge* (1937)
HarperCollins · Hb · 256pp · £9.99 · ISBN 9780008314293

suggested, it was the snobbery attached to anything foreign-sounding – just as the ballerina Miss Jones had to become Miss Joneova and Mr Robinson the tenor became Signor Robinelli. Perhaps it was the lack of legal protection given to British brand names. At any rate, his request in London restaurants for Cheshire cheese had produced either no cheese at all or merely a soapy substance imported under the trade designation of 'Cheshire', which was a libel on that cheese. 'Do people really want to go to the Dorchester to be given the choice of Camembert or Gorgonzola?' he asked. Perhaps the fault lay with modern urban housekeeping, the willingness of 'labour-saving wives to get anything out of a labour-saving tin, or a silver-paper packet'. Finally, Squire suggested that a statue be erected to Mrs Paulet of Wymondham, the inventor of Stilton, 'this noble fragrant cheese, the cheese of poets'. He was ready to start a fund . . . He duly became chairman of the Stilton Memorial Committee.

T. S. Eliot was a fellow cheese-lover. 'Never commit yourself to a cheese without having first . . . *examined* it,' he told a friend. He had long regarded Squire as a hopeless reactionary but he replied, praising Squire for his 'manly and spirited defence' of Stilton. He nevertheless contested its claims to pre-eminence: Wensleydale, not Stilton, was the 'Mozart of cheeses'. In any case, a statue was not a good idea: a Society for the Preservation of Ancient Cheeses was the way forward. (Squire was a keen member of a whole range of conservation societies, including the Society for the Protection of Ancient Buildings.) 'But this is no time for disputes between eaters of English cheese,' Eliot wrote, 'the situation is precarious and we must stick together.' The appreciation of cheese was perhaps the only thing upon which the two men could agree.

The correspondence in *The Times* and the publication in 1936 of Osbert Burdett's *Little Book of Cheese* suggested to Squire another venture. He invited a group of friends and writers to contribute a chapter each to a book championing their favourite cheese. In 1937 *Cheddar Gorge* was published at 10s 6d, with a collectors' edition of fifty copies at 10 guineas. Ernest Shepard provided the illustrations, some in the comic style of his work for *Punch*, others offering a lyrical view of country life and customs. Squire thought these 'quite lovely, far better than his Christopher Robin stuff'.

In his introduction Squire noted the decline of British cheeses. Many had already disappeared. Some, he granted, were not to be regretted – 'a man who ate Suffolk cheese might as well be chewing old motor tyres' – but many were real losses. The problem was ignorance. To redress this, each contributor was sent off to tour their local region, visit farmers and dairies, and talk to the cheesemakers, who were nearly always farmers' wives. *Cheddar Gorge* records a series of journeys through England from Devon to Yorkshire, and beyond. There are visits to the notable inns and clubs where cheese was to be enjoyed: the Cheshire Cheese in Fleet Street, the Bell at Stilton and the Boar's Head at Caerphilly. Squire himself wrote on Stilton, 'the King of Cheeses'. The praises of Scotland's only cheese, the fast disappearing Ayrshire Dunlop, were sung by Moray McLaren. The Irish poet and nationalist Oliver St John Gogarty wanted to reclaim the names of the genuine Irish cheeses of Ardagh, Galtee and Whitehorn, whose true identities were concealed under 'Irish' Cheddar or 'Irish' Stilton. Cheese, he suggested, had a 'peaceful and soporific effect' which would promote friendship between nations.

Vyvyan Holland, Oscar Wilde's son, chose Cheshire, a truly British cheese as it came in three colours – red, white and blue. Osbert Burdett wrote of the May Day celebrations in Randwick, near Stroud, when three large Gloucester cheeses, garlanded with flowers, were paraded through the village and serenaded by the local band. The first cuts from them were distributed to all the young maids in the neighbourhood as a kind of fertility rite.

Science, history, recipes and anecdotes are woven together in *Cheddar Gorge*. Some of Squire's contributors write in detail about the chemistry of cheese production and muse on the making of rennet. The food writer André Simon provides a chemical analysis of the nearly extinct Blue Vinny from Dorset. Farmers in the county told him that its mysterious colour came from leaving it to mature beside mouldy old leather shoes and harnesses. There is the tale of the venerable Stilton that purred like a cat when stroked, and the story of a well-known Manchester cheese factor who always bought the cheese the mice had been at since they were the best judges.

Ernest H. Shepard, 'The best judges of good cheese'

Many stories are told of cheeses of legendary size. The then biggest cheese in the world, a gargantuan Cheddar weighing around 550 kilogrammes, was presented to Queen Victoria. In 1909 a prize-winning Cheshire weighing 200lbs was given to her son Edward VII. The following year Mr Percy Cooke of Tattenhall farm near Chester delivered an order for twenty Cheshire cheeses with a combined weight of two and a half tons. One monstrous cheese was big enough to contain a 13-year-old child.

Several of Sir John's contributors discuss Welsh Rarebit and earn his scorn for using the term – 'a vile modern refinement of Welsh Rabbit'. The popular novelist Horace Annersley Vachell was given the recipe grudgingly by his aunt, who made him promise to keep it secret. A friend badgered him to make it. He gave her a list of the ingredients (including a confusing extra two or three he had no intention of actually using) and prepared the dish behind a tall screen. The result was delicious – but when she tried to recreate the recipe it was a disaster. The secret stayed with him until after his aunt's death, but at last he could now share the recipe:

> Cut half a pound of Cheddar Cheese into thin slices and put them in a stew pan. Add three tablespoonsful of milk and a gill of cream, the yolks of three eggs and the whites of two. Season with pepper and salt.
>
> Whip it until it boils – and it is done.
>
> Let your guests be handed squares of toast. Let the cheese be served in a dish. The guests will spread the hot cheese on the hot toast . . .

Many of Squire's contributors had strong views about how cheese should be served. His friend Henry Stevens enjoyed eating Leicester with sweet 'pin-money' onions, but Leicester and watercress were the ideal combination. Ambrose Heath thought that celery or celery salt might go with Stilton or Cheshire, but that Wensleydale was best served with no accompaniments except perhaps a few plain leaves of lamb's lettuce. Dieticians of the time warned against the 'providential' combination of bread and cheese, but Vyvyan Holland told his readers not to listen to the 'peevish vapourings of the jealous dyspeptic'.

And then there was the question of what to drink with cheese. Port was traditional with Stilton. Cheddar and vintage port were 'Heavenly Twins' and promised health and longevity, wrote Horace Vachell, but the Scot Moray McLaren warned against it – 'a rich, sweet, English drink', fine in its place but offensive at the end of a meal. 'English cheeses are plain fellows better suited to a plain oaken table, a clean cloth and a tankard,' wrote the food writer Ambrose Heath. 'Beer or burgundy to my thinking; but, better still, water, and whatever you like afterwards,' prescribed Sir John.

Above all, *Cheddar Gorge* reflects Squire's own love of all things rural and traditional. A doughty campaigner, he was best known for saving Stonehenge from being surrounded by commercial building. He fought to preserve the countryside from the car and the ribbon development of the 1920s and '30s. The cheese board was his battleground in miniature. He sided with the small farmer against the factory; the native against the foreign; the art of cheese-making against the product of the white-clad scientist; the tasty against the bland.

His defence of British cheese was one campaign which was entirely successful. When *Cheddar Gorge* was published, no British cheese was being exported. Squire would have been amazed to hear that eighty years on there were more than 750 types of British cheese and the export trade was worth £615 million.

JOHN SMART lives in an old pub in Norfolk. He has written on John Hayward and T. S. Eliot, and on Modernism and twentieth-century drama, and is currently writing a life of Sir John Squire.

A Strangulation of the Soul

MAGGIE FERGUSSON

It was dusk on a winter's day, many years ago now, when I settled down to read the prison letters of Dennis Nilsen, the most prolific murderer in British history. They had been donated to the Royal Society of Literature, where I worked, to raise money at an auction at Sotheby's, and they were chilling. Written in hard-pressed-down black biro, the words were crammed on the pages with no breathing space – a graphologist had described them as indicating 'a strangulation of the soul' – and they bristled with contempt and fury against everything and everyone. But Nilsen's critical savagery was never turned on himself – strange, as he had fatally strangled fifteen men.

The letters had come from, and were addressed to, Brian Masters. At the time of Nilsen's arrest in 1983, Masters was known as the biographer of Georgiana, Duchess of Devonshire, John Aspinall and E. F. Benson, among others. But when, one breakfast time, he read a newspaper report of the arrest of Dennis Nilsen, he was intrigued. First, here was a man who loved Shakespeare, Elgar, Mahler, Tchaikovsky, Sibelius – but who had repeatedly killed in cold blood, and then stashed the bodies under his floorboards. Second, what did it say about society, and specifically about the drifting shoals of homosexuals eddying around pubs in central London, that so many men could disappear off the face of the earth, and never be missed? So Masters wrote to Nilsen, and swiftly received a reply: 'Dear Mr Masters, I pass the burden of my life onto your shoulder.' This was

Brian Masters, *Killing for Company* (1985)
Arrow · Pb · 368pp · £8.99 · ISBN 9781784759421

how *Killing for Company* (1985) began. I am not a connoisseur of true-crime literature, but this book – consistently in print now for thirty-five years – is surely a classic.

What I admire most about Brian Masters's writing is its restraint. A certain amount of grim detail is necessary in telling the tale, but Masters never gloats over it. Early on in his research, the police offered to show him around a hundred photographs of the body parts they had discovered in Nilsen's attic flat. After eleven, he could look no more: his appetite for horror was limited. He never uses tabloid 'trigger' words like 'repellent', 'disgusting', 'horrifying'. His style is more Dostoevsky than *Daily Mail*. He hopes not to shock, but to comprehend Nilsen's place in the 'jumbled kaleidoscope of the human condition'. And because he remains, in his own words, 'a relatively quiet narrator', readers are 'obliged to use their imagination in order to provide the shocks which I neglected'. Not surprising, then, that after the book was published, many people wrote to Masters to say they no longer dared switch off their bedroom lights at night.

The drama begins on the freezing, snowy morning of 9 February 1983 – which Nilsen later described as 'the day that help arrived'. Nilsen arrived home from work – he was employed at a JobCentre in Kentish Town – to find two policemen waiting for him. He had, in fact, engineered his own arrest by writing to the landlord of his flat at 23 Cranley Gardens, Muswell Hill, to complain of blocked drains. On investigating, Michael Cattran, a plumber from DynoRod and new to the business, found that the drains were clogged up with slimy quantities of human flesh. Nilsen told the policemen that if they would just take him to the police station, he would explain everything – 'I want to get it all off my chest.' In the car, DCI Peter Jay asked, 'Are we talking about one body or two?' 'Fifteen,' said Nilsen, killed over nearly five years.

During the ensuing thirty hours of interviews, the whole grisly story tumbled out. If Nilsen showed no remorse, he also astonished the police by going to great lengths to help them with their inquiry. He told them where, exactly, they might find body parts in his flat: in a wardrobe, a tea chest, under the bath, under the floorboards. Masters is good at detail: these corpses had not been cut up with a knife and stuffed into carrier bags, they had been cut up with 'a long kitchen knife with a brown handle' and stowed in bags from Woolworths. The large bones had been put out with the rubbish; the heads, most difficult to dispose of, had been boiled down in a large cooking pot Nilsen had originally bought to do the catering for an office party, and had later used as a home for goldfish.

At his trial, Nilsen expressed surprise that anyone should find these details upsetting – 'a corpse is a thing, and it cannot hurt or suffer'; the men he had murdered were now 'beyond pain, problems and sorrow'. But the jury didn't see it like this. Some felt so physically ill they were barely able to stay in their seats. 'I remember a woman in the front row . . . staring at him in the dock with visible blunt incredulity,' writes Masters, 'unable to attach the bureaucrat before her to the evidence she was hearing.' Yet Nilsen was not only adjudged sane but also ruled not to be suffering from diminished responsibility. 'I am an ordinary man,' he said of himself, 'come to an extraordinary conclusion.' Dr Bowen, the psychiatrist brought in to assess him, admitted that he 'felt strong sympathy for the defendant'.

In an email correspondence with Masters, during lockdown, I asked whether he had liked Nilsen. He had, after all, continued to visit him for years after the trial, and after the book was published – up until the moment, in fact, when Nilsen decided to cut him off. No, said Masters, he never liked him, and 'he would never have been a friend in the normal happenstance'. Despite this, he believed that Nilsen was not a 'stranger among us', but 'an extreme instance of human possibility'. 'If he were a monster,' Masters writes, 'we should learn nothing by studying his deplorable behaviour; it is because he is also human that we must make the attempt.' What drove him on as he wrote the book was an urge to understand, if imperfectly, 'one dark and mysterious aspect of the human condition'; what forces had been at work to disfigure Nilsen's emotional grasp of the world about him.

And so Masters plunges back into Nilsen's Scottish childhood, in the fishing village of Strichen in Aberdeenshire, where he grew up in a community 'turned in on itself', and troubled with much mental disorder. Nilsen never once met his Norwegian father, and his mother, Betty, admitted to Masters that she had felt unable ever to cuddle her son – 'he seemed to repel demonstrations of affection'. And so he became 'a "skowkie" child, unsmiling and resentful of questioning by adults, to whom he gave a clear impression of distrust and reserve'. His one true companion was his maternal grandfather, Andrew Whyte; but Whyte died when Dennis Nilsen was not yet 6, and at this point, Masters believes, 'death and love' became entangled in his mind.

As a cadet in the Army Catering Corps, where his conduct was considered 'exemplary', Nilsen learned his butchering skills. Then, after brief service in the police force, he joined the Civil Service, employed initially at a JobCentre in Denmark Street, Soho. The staff working with him considered him good-humoured, straightforward and kind – he once baked a birthday cake for a colleague nobody much liked – but some conceded that there was 'a lingering hint of despair about him', and he later admitted that, even in company, he felt desperately alone. He had by now accepted his homosexuality, but anonymous sex, easily available, only aggravated his sense of 'corrosive loneliness'.

On 30 December 1978, at the Cricklewood Arms, Nilsen picked up an Irish youth, 14-year-old Stephen Holmes. He took him back home and welcomed him into his bed. At first light, Nilsen woke and strangled Holmes. 'I had started down the avenue of death,' he later wrote, 'and possession of a new kind of flat-mate.'

All fifteen of Nilsen's victims were strangled – but that was only the beginning. After they were dead, he would whisper to them 'words of solace': he felt he had 'somehow released them'. Then he would bathe them, dress them, cuddle up with them on the sofa, listen to classical music, chat. He told the police that he did not consider himself a murderer, 'although I have killed'. And asked by his solicitor why he had done what he had, he replied: 'I am hoping you will tell me that.'

And yet to Brian Masters, in masses of letters and fifty prison notebooks crammed with reminiscence and reflection, Nilsen got as close as he could to revealing himself. 'All of us conceal in conversation clues to personalities which we happily reveal on paper,' he wrote, 'because the added distance of writing lends protection and encourages the risks of intimacy.' To Masters, Nilsen was able to explain that he had been 'killing for company'.

In the end, Sotheby's wouldn't touch Nilsen's letters, and they were returned to Brian Masters. We're now several years on from Nilsen's death in HMP Full Sutton, and it unsettled me to think that Masters might still be living with this macabre package of correspondence. But no, he says; he's not. The letters are in a bank vault and will eventually pass to the librarian at the Garrick Club. 'I don't know what David Garrick would have made of that,' says Masters. 'But some of my fellow members in the acting profession will appreciate the haul.'

MAGGIE FERGUSSON is Literary Editor of the Catholic weekly *The Tablet*, where she keeps her appetite for murder under wraps.

The Price of Virtue

FRANCES DONNELLY

Hotel du Lac was Anita Brookner's fourth novel, published in 1984. To the consternation of many and the incredulity of the author, it won the Booker Prize that year. The photograph taken after the announcement shows an author wide-eyed with disbelief. And not just Ms Brookner. One of the judges, the late great Sir Malcolm Bradbury, consoled Julian Barnes, also shortlisted, with the words: 'Bad luck, Julian – the wrong book won.' With the greatest respect, Sir Malcolm, there are those of us who disagree. *Hotel du Lac* is the work of a supremely gifted novelist at the top of her game. Not just elegant, insightful and thought-provoking, but still, after many readings, laugh-out-loud funny. So it is pleasing to know from a work colleague that, for the whole of the next day, Anita was completely elated.

Bear in mind that writing novels was her second brilliant career. She was born in Herne Hill in 1928 to Polish Jewish parents whose original name was Bruckner. Her upbringing, though comfortable, was not happy. A First in Art History led to a doctorate at the Courtauld, then ten years in Paris – 'the happiest time of my life'. Later, in 1987, she became the first female Slade Professor of Fine Arts at Cambridge. She loved teaching and was a revered and respected tutor.

But by the time she was 50, some reassessment was being made. She was on her own. There had been proposals but none had seemed right. In her most laconic style she commented: 'Men have their own agenda.

Anita Brookner, *Hotel du Lac* (1984)
Penguin · Pb · 192pp · £8.99 · ISBN 9780140147476

They think you can be made to fit in with their lives if they lop off certain parts of yours. You can see them coming a mile off.' Immensely private, she had a wonderful way of deflecting enquiries about her personal life by uttering oracular statements so bald as to silence the enquirer – 'I could probably go into the *Guinness Book of Records* as the loneliest woman in London' being one. But one hot London summer she began to write fiction, beginning aptly enough with *A Start in Life* (1981). She wanted to analyse the paths that had led to

© The Estate of Chris Garnham/
National Portrait Gallery, London

her present isolation. With a typical flourish of bravado she remarked, 'I thought of my lost hopes and how lucky I was to be able to convert them so easily into satire.' But that is a characteristic piece of self-deprecation. Her novels are sympathetic, witty and scrupulously truthful. Lucidity was both her goal and her great gift to her readers. Her books appear understated yet are capable of delivering their own deep emotional shocks.

Hotel du Lac remains Anita Brookner's most popular novel and the one in which she most clearly sets out the ideas underlying her work. Its first-person narrator is a woman called Edith Hope who makes her living by writing romantic fiction 'under a more thrusting name'. She lives off the Fulham Road and describes herself as a discreet and responsible person: she pays her taxes on time and never rings her publisher. But she has done something neither discreet nor responsible – which has necessitated an enforced holiday at the Hotel du Lac near Geneva. This is a luxury hotel with excellent food and wonderful service, yet it is low-key to the point of inaudibility. There are no organized activities, no disco, no tempting glass cases full of luxury goods. There is an uninviting bar which everyone voluntarily leaves after one drink. Yet you need a recommendation to book a room here. It is revealed not as a house of correction, more a remittance house to which people are sent after emotional or chemical incontinence. Edith has committed a social gaffe and has come here to expatiate her sins.

The 'crime' is revealed halfway through the book. A week before her summary departure to Switzerland she had been about to marry. But on her wedding day, approaching the Registry Office and viewing her future husband, she had had a change of heart and had quietly told her driver to drive on. It is a superlative scene of high comedy: the guests in large hats surge expectantly towards Edith's car, then all heads slowly swivel in disbelief as it disappears off up the King's Road.

Not much fun for the would-be bridegroom, though. 'Edith, you have made a fool of me,' he later says with some dignity. 'Geoffrey,' she replies, 'I think you will find I have made a fool only of myself.' The problem is that though Geoffrey has an excellent flat in Montagu Square – he'd lived there with his mother – he does not have Edith's heart. That is bestowed on a foxy married man called David who comes round once a month for extramarital sex followed by egg and chips. ('I am a good plain cook.') She is used to listening to the sound of his departing car, then returning, with an aching heart, to her writing.

Edith's romantic novels, though clearly lucrative, are hard to place – probably not Mills & Boon (she writes with a fountain pen), yet certainly not Having-It-All tales of the 1980s. At the beginning of the book her agent even hints that she may have to up her game – 'the romantic market is beginning to change. It's sex for the young woman executive, the *Cosmopolitan* reader.'

But Edith is completely unmoved. 'Most women', she tells him, 'prefer the old myths. Particularly Aesop's fable of the Tortoise and the Hare. Because the tortoise wins every time, just as in my books. The mouse-like unassuming girl gets the hero. It is a lie,' she adds pleasantly. 'In reality the hare always wins. But not in fiction. At least, not in mine. My readers are essentially virtuous.'

During her time at the Hotel du Lac she ponders deeply as to what behaviour most becomes a woman, and there seems to be no satisfactory conclusion. Virtue does seem, in real life, to be entirely its own reward mainly because no one else – especially men – appears to have a blind bit of interest in it. On the contrary, it's the louder voices of the shallow, the greedy and the self-regarding that seem to ensure the most interest and attention. Reality is ordinary women struggling to make lives for themselves or trying to make peace with the life they have.

And yet. There are proposals. Towards the end of the book Edith remarks, with consternation: 'I have received two proposals of marriage this year and I seem to have accepted both of them.' But she declines both: she cannot commit where her heart is not engaged. Quite wrong, Anita Brookner later robustly remarks. 'She should have accepted one of them.' As a married woman Edith would have had status and a place in society. In the absence of Prince Charming, an older Brookner felt this was an equitable bargain.

The search for love and usually the failure to find it (the sole exception is *The Bay of Angels* (2001) and even then the heroine sees the beloved for only six months of the year) is a dominant Brookner theme. Some critics have suggested that she wrote the same book again and again. 'Of course,' she replied crushingly. 'All writers do.' But few with as much truthfulness, humour and sympathy.

FRANCES DONNELLY still lives happily in Suffolk. One of her goals during lockdown was to rehome a dog from a rescue centre, but she discovered that too many other people had had the same idea. She is currently thinking of rehoming a cat.

The Tolkien Test

KEN HAIGH

As parents, we hope our children will love the books we ourselves enjoyed, the ones that turned us into readers. But as often as not, our attempts to interest them fail. I remember a friend who was disappointed he couldn't get his grandchildren to share his love of *Swallows and Amazons*, a book that had had a huge influence on his life, one that had turned him into a weekend sailor, even encouraged him to build his own boat.

'What went wrong?' I asked.

'They found it impossible to take the book seriously.'

'Why?'

'Well,' – he reddened – 'because it has a character named Titty. That might pass in the UK, but not here in Canada.'

My own Waterloo came with *The Hobbit*. Try as I might, I could not get my children interested. My own introduction to Tolkien had come in Mrs White's grade five/six classroom. At the end of each school day, as a reward for good behaviour, Mrs White would gather her pupils in a semi-circle on the carpet and read to us. This was our favourite part of the day. Over the course of two years, she gradually worked her way through Enid Blyton's adventure stories but then, toward the end of my final year in primary school, she announced she was going to try something new.

She gathered us together as usual and began to read. It was as if an electric current had gone through the room. We sat up straighter. We

J. R. R. Tolkien, *The Hobbit* (1937)

HarperCollins · Hb · 320pp · £20 · ISBN 9780261103283

pricked up our ears. We had never heard anything like this before: trolls and dwarves, wizards and elves, magic rings and giant spiders, and not told like a fairy story, but written as if it had really happened. We loved it. Each day we rushed through our school work so that we could savour these last fifteen minutes of the school day.

Then the unthinkable happened. We reached the last day of term and she closed the book, unfinished, and wished us all a pleasant summer holiday. I immediately rushed to the public library, took out a copy and finished it. Then I started again, from the beginning.

What was the appeal of *The Hobbit*? Oh, where to start? There was the dangerous quest for one thing, complete with dragons and a whimsical map. (Maps are important.) There was the gathering of a band of brothers, that common theme of male adventure novels which, when you stop to think about it, is also the appeal of Robin Hood and King Arthur. And then there was the creation of a truly realized fantasy world with its own history, folklore and language.

No one had done this before, at least not on this level. Only later would I realize that Tolkien had borrowed many of his ideas from his study of Old English tales like *Beowulf* and the Old Norse *Eddur*. For me personally, a boy who loved fishing and camping, it was Tolkien's obvious love of the outdoors that appealed. Tolkien loved trees. Think of all the great forests in Middle Earth – Lothlórien, Fangorn, the Old Forest and Mirkwood.

And then there was the journey itself. Even as a child, I think I knew that all the best journeys were made by shanks's pony, and *The Hobbit*, with its subtitle, *There and Back Again*, is, above all, the diary of a long journey undertaken on foot. As a boy, I would lie in bed at night and imagine my own adventures, staff in hand, rucksack on my back, walking through the dark forests of Middle Earth.

In retrospect, however, I think it was the creation of the hobbits themselves that impressed me most. They are likeable heroes – not brave or strong, perhaps even a bit silly, but resilient and resourceful. They are like children, in fact. Hobbits overindulge in the simple things they enjoy most, like eating, drinking, smoking their pipes and singing. Hobbits, I think, embody the kind of virtues Tolkien saw in the average Englishman: kindness, determination, stewardship (so many of his heroes are gardeners) and fidelity, the sort of virtues that were worth fighting for, and which, when challenged, the common man would step up to preserve. For despite many temptations to abandon the quest, in the end the little hobbit Bilbo masters his fear and shows true courage. This is the sort of lesson a child unknowingly absorbs.

But back to my original point: how to interest my children in *The Hobbit*? Was it even fair to force the novel on them? I decided to take a leaf out of Mrs White's book. One day, while they were idly drawing or playing with Lego, I opened *The Hobbit* and began to read aloud, pretending the children weren't even in the room:

> In a hole in the ground there lived a hobbit. Not a nasty, dirty, wet hole, filled with the ends of worms and an oozy smell, nor

yet a dry, bare, sandy hole with nothing in it to sit down on or to eat: it was a hobbit-hole, and that means comfort.

After the first page or so, my daughter put aside what she was doing and snuggled up next to me on the sofa. The boys were still building weapons of mass destruction, but I noticed their hands weren't moving quite as quickly. They were pausing from time to time, distracted. After a few more pages, I sighed dramatically and shut the book.

'What are you doing?' my daughter said. 'Don't stop.'

'What? You want me to keep going?'

'Yes,' they all replied.

'But I thought you didn't want to read *The Hobbit?*'

'Well, we'll try a *bit* more, just to see if it's any good.'

So all three of them draped themselves on the sofa, and I went on reading. Each night thereafter we carried on until we'd finished the book.

Now this was some years ago, before *The Hobbit* was turned into a bloated trilogy of films. After seeing them, one of my sons decided to read the book again, this time on his own. I asked him how it compared.

He looked thoughtful. 'The films missed the point. *The Hobbit* isn't an epic, like *The Lord of the Rings*. It's a simple story. The movies didn't need to get so long and complicated. In fact, the best scenes in the movie were taken straight from the book.'

Out of the mouths of babes.

KEN HAIGH is a librarian from Canada who misses the days when his children were small enough to curl up in his lap and be read to.

Winston and Clementine

JANE RIDLEY

It was lockdown, and I was short of a book to read. One night I picked up the fat paperback volume of letters that I had ordered from Amazon (yes, I know, but where else could I buy a 1999 paperback in twenty-four hours in the panicky first weeks of the pandemic?). The book was *Speaking for Themselves: The Personal Letters of Winston and Clementine Churchill*; I thought it might be useful research for my biography of King George V. To my surprise, I was gripped. During those early weeks of London lockdown, I clung to the certainty of routine: long walks through the haunted, empty streets of Mayfair or Westminster, sneaking in two walks a day because of my dog, the weekly socially distanced supermarket queue and, at the end of those strange housebound days, looking forward to my bedtime ration of Churchill letters.

Churchill was a stunningly prolific writer. An article such as I am writing now of 1,800 words, which is long by our standards, he would toss off in a couple of hours. According to an American website, he wrote an estimated 20 million words in his lifetime. A very large proportion of the words he wrote are about himself, even the books purporting to be historical. Of *The World Crisis*, Churchill's history of the First World War, A. J. Balfour observed that it was 'Winston's brilliant autobiography, disguised as a history of the universe'. The eight volumes of the official Churchill biography by Martin Gilbert

Mary Soames (ed.), *Speaking for Themselves: The Personal Letters of Winston and Clementine Churchill* (1999)
Black Swan · Pb · 768pp · £25 · ISBN 9780552997508

total 3 million words, and these volumes of biography were accompanied by twenty-three companion volumes of printed documents and letters, which add another 12 million words.

The effect of all these millions of published words is to bury Churchill, making him less accessible rather than more so. No one today is going to plough through all eight volumes of Gilbert's official biography, magisterial and comprehensive though it is. Andrew Roberts's terrific 2018 biography fills a gap by constructing a narrative of Churchill's life which works for readers of today (and even that weighs in at over 1,100 pages).

This rich collection of 1,700 letters between Winston and Clementine, written over a marriage of fifty-six years, was edited by Churchill's daughter Mary Soames in 1999. The letters formed the core material for her bestselling 1979 biography of her mother. Inevitably the correspondence is uneven. The Churchills wrote to one another when they were apart, and this means that at times such as the Second World War, when they were mainly together, there is relatively little material. Mary Soames's editing is very well judged. She tells you what you need to know without overloading and obscuring the text with unnecessary detail.

The joy of the Winston/Clementine letters is that you can hear Churchill and his wife almost as they speak. The letters are not weighed down by the bombast and booming rhetoric of some of Churchill's published work. Nor are they mediated through the lens of a historian or a biographer. In these letters you get your Churchill neat, and the immediacy brings you closer to the man than many of the books about him.

Churchill married Clementine Hozier in 1908 when he was 33 and already a Cabinet minister. Clementine was ten years younger. As a young man, Churchill was widely disliked by his contemporaries on account of his insufferable cockiness, but in his letters to Clementine he was neither arrogant nor overbearing. On the contrary, he claimed to be

'stupid & clumsy' in his relations with women, and he described himself as a loner – 'a solitary figure in the midst of crowds'. He told her: 'I am so much centred in my politics, that often I must be a dull companion.' He found in Clementine an equal and a supporter. 'Don't be disloyal to me in thought,' he begged her, 'I have no one but you to break the loneliness of a bustled & bustling existence.' To which she replied: 'What I want & enjoy is that you should feel quite comfortable and at home with me.'

The tipping point in this lifelong conversation comes with the First World War. For Winston the outbreak of war was the moment he had been preparing for ever since as a boy he had played with thousands of lead soldiers. 'I know how you are feeling,' wrote Clementine in July 1914, 'tingling with life to the tips of your fingers.' But the disastrous failure of the Dardanelles expedition led to his disgrace and resignation, and he left the government to join the army in France. From the front, Winston poured out his feelings in letters to Clementine – 'I had almost lost the Art of writing,' he wrote. 'I am gradually regaining it through my missives to you.' These are marvellous letters, the descriptions informed by an acute under-standing of warfare. As Clementine wrote, 'How much better you describe things than the most brilliant news-paper correspondent. But I forget. You were one once.'

There can be few men for whom the experience of the trenches was a rest cure, but Churchill claimed that under fire he found 'tranquillity', happiness and release from care. He writhed daily, however, at 'the lack of power to make things work'. Marginalized and powerless, he looked on with dismay. 'I see so much that ought to be done . . . that will never be done.' One of the most striking themes to emerge from these letters is Churchill's sense of destiny and his bomb-proof self-belief. In spite of the collapse of his political stock after the Dardanelles, he ached to return home and take a share in the direction of the war. From London Clementine wrote warning him repeatedly against taking the 'awful risk' of coming back lonely and unprotected. '*For once only* I pray be patient.' For once he listened.

I read these letters in sections, dotting around rather than working chronologically through them. Those from the 1920s and '30s are especially good. By then Churchill had returned to the Conservative party, but he certainly wasn't the hunting, shooting, fishing type of Tory. He liked to spend the winter months in the South of France with rich friends such as Consuelo ex-Duchess of Marlborough or the Duke of Westminster, and visit the casinos there – 'it excites me so much to play – foolish moth'. Perhaps he needed the thrill: gambling was for him a substitute for political crisis. He was never happier than when fighting an emergency such as the 1926 General Strike – 'an anxious but a thrilling & engrossing time with power & scope which is what the Pig likes', as Clementine described it. How he would have enjoyed fighting the pandemic.

Money was a constant worry. Churchill relied on his pen to pay the bills, and the letters give a vivid sense of living from one deadline to the next. Whenever he had money he spent it. In 1921 he inherited a fortune from a distant relative, which seemingly freed him from the need to earn money by writing articles at inconvenient times. Not so. By 1926 he was once more on his uppers. 'No more champagne!' he cried, and proposed drastic economies such as letting Chartwell and cutting down to two clean white shirts a week.

When the Conservative government fell in 1929 and Churchill was in opposition, he plunged at once into work on the life of his ancestor, the great Duke of Marlborough. At one point he was churning out 20,000 words a week. Most of what he wrote after 1918 was dictated to a secretary (always a Miss), and his letters to Clementine were dictated as well. 'I have almost lost the art of thinking with a pen in my hand.'

Churchill was a loyal, devoted and affectionate husband, but he and Clementine had little in common. They shared an interest in politics, but she remained staunchly Liberal while he moved to the right. She liked the sea and

was a talented tennis player. He preferred painting. She was sociable and enjoyed visiting friends, he was happiest at home at Chartwell. Here he spent his time dictating, bricklaying and supervising a small, uneconomic farm, and all the while 'I drink champagne at all meals and buckets of claret & soda in between.' This was the Chartwell dream, and it was not a life that Clementine greatly enjoyed.

Churchill's sheer energy and his need for constant drama and activity were exhausting. Little wonder that Clementine sometimes found the pace of life with him too much. His gambling frightened her. Gambling had destroyed her family. It had made her 'ill and ashamed' to watch her mother Blanche Hozier tottering down to the casino in Dieppe and recklessly flinging away her money at chemin de fer in a 'superstitious and groping' manner. Scarred by this, Clementine was more risk-averse than Winston. She was a worrier. 'It is a great fault in me that small things should have the power to harass & agonize me.'

She travelled often, and her letters are sometimes written from nursing homes or health farms where she took herself to cure her nervous collapse and extreme fatigue. She was a neglectful mother; looking after Winston was more than enough. Some have commented that the real cause of Clementine's nerves was the need to get away from her hyperactive husband.

Clementine was no doormat. If she thought Winston was wrong she told him so. She usually wrote him a letter, even if they were in the same house, because she knew she would lose an argument with him in person. In 1940 she roundly rebuked him for his 'rough and sarcastic manner' towards his private secretaries and his 'contemptuous' manner towards his colleagues. 'My Darling Winston,' she wrote, 'I must confess that I have noticed a deterioration in your manner; & you are not so kind as you used to be.' On his frequent journeys during the war to secret destinations, she insisted – rightly as it turned out – that he be accompanied by a doctor. She watched his flights with anxiety, sending telegrams in code: 'Mrs Frankland to Air Commodore Frankland. I am following your movements with intense interest, the cage is swept and garnished fresh water and hemp seed are temptingly displayed, the door is open and it is hoped that soon Mr Bullfinch will fly home.'

Churchill resigned as Prime Minister in 1955 aged 80, and he lived on until 1965. These forgotten last years are charted in the letters he wrote from the Riviera, gambling in the casino, dictating and painting – 'a wonderful cure because you really cannot think of anything else'.

Without these intimate letters the private side of Churchill would be unknowable. Churchill kept no diary, and this lifelong exchange brings us closer than anything else to an extraordinary human being.

JANE RIDLEY is working on a biography of King George V and Queen Mary.

The decorations that appear in the margins are taken from letters by Winston and Clementine.

Innocent or Not?

CHRISTIAN TYLER

Chance put this book into my hands – and I shall be forever grateful to her.

Searching for local colour from late seventeenth-century Rome for a project of my own, I came across the Italian historical thriller *Imprimatur* (2002) by Rita Monaldi and Francesco Sorti. Whodunnits are not really my thing, but this seemed likely to fit the bill. It had been a hit all over Europe and was favourably compared with Umberto Eco's *The Name of the Rose*.

Then I read that the Vatican had been accused of leaning on Italian publishers to boycott further editions of the novel because of its controversial claims about the Pope of that time, Innocent XI. Given the Catholic Church's history of banning books, there was an appealing irony here. The book's title, *Imprimatur*, means 'Let it be printed' and is the Church's official stamp of approval for theologically vetted works. But the controversy – so it was said – had done even greater damage: it had forced the Congregation for the Causes of Saints to suspend Pope Innocent's imminent canonization.

All this was intriguing, but it looked suspect. The book's authors, Rita Monaldi and Francesco Sorti, are a married couple and both former journalists. The Vatican, being the world's oldest extant institution, is a favourite (and sometimes deserving) target of the press. But I know Italian (and British) journalists who have written books

Rita Monaldi & Francesco Sorti, *Imprimatur* (2002, English edition 2008) ·
Trans. Peter Burnett
Birlinn · Pb · 666pp · £9.99 · ISBN 9781846972645

in which far worse things have been said about it, without hindrance. Besides, the controversy was not new.

The issue is whether Pope Innocent, while still Cardinal Benedetto Odescalchi, had directed his family's merchant bank to lend large sums to the Protestant William of Orange. The money was to fund William's wars against the Catholic King Louis XIV of France, but it may also have enabled William's coup against another Catholic monarch, James II of England, in 1688. In short, the loans were seen as treachery amounting almost to heresy.

Once pope, Innocent showed himself unusually ascetic, shutting theatres, cracking down on public indecency, suppressing graft and living – like the present Pope Francis – in the humblest quarters of the papal palace. More to the point, he actively mobilized European resistance to the encroaching Ottoman Turks who were encamped under the walls of Vienna.

Innocent was put up for canonization in 1741 but progress was interrupted by French complaints and accusations of secret Jansenist leanings. His beatification, the stage before sainthood, was reached only under Pius XII in 1956. In 2003, under the Polish pope John Paul II (himself now a saint), there was rumoured to be a move to get Innocent XI's cause over the line as a way of showing defiance in the face of the 9/11 attacks on America by Islamic fundamentalists. But that sounds improbable. John Paul was noted for building bridges with orthodox Islam as well as other faiths.

All this background is interesting, but the book has no need of extravagant promotion. It stands on its own.

The date is September 1683, and we are in a *locanda* in the Via dell'Orso just north of the Piazza Navona and close to the Tiber. The ten guests, the innkeeper and his young apprentice are being locked in following the unexplained death of one of the lodgers, an old Frenchman. The authorities suspect the plague. Officers arrive and take the names of the inmates, many of whom (as we will learn) are not quite what they pretend to be, including the young courtesan

Cloridia who is the only woman in the place. A claustrophobic setting then, but rather appropriate, since I picked up the book just as
we were entering the first coronavirus lockdown.

The story is told by the 20-year-old apprentice, whose diary we are
purportedly reading. He is small – perhaps a dwarf – uneducated but
intelligent enough to ask all the questions we need answered in order
to follow the plot.

When the apprentice discovers that three little pearls given him by
one of the guests have been stolen, he is helped by another inmate,
Atto Melani, a former castrato chorister and 'honorary abbot' who
has been on the payroll of Louis XIV. Their joint search uncovers a
secret staircase which leads them through dripping passages down to
the halls and sewers of ancient Rome where they meet, amid the
scurrying rats, a couple of *corpisantari* or relic-hunters who scratch a
living by selling pieces of bone supposedly belonging to early
Christian martyrs. Ugonio speaks in mangled malapropisms while
his mate Ciacconio can only mumble something that sounds like
'Gfrrrlubh'. They may be revolting, but the *corpisantari* have hearts
of gold and, in a story replete with villains, they are the heroes.

While the nights are spent peering through the dark, the days bring
relief and growing comprehension – for us, the readers, as much as for
the narrator – as the apprentice and his cunning mentor Melani go
over what they have learned the previous night. Beguiled by the young
man's innocence, the other inmates also drop hints. And so unfolds a
panoptic view of political intrigue embracing all of Europe.

A Muslim invasion is threatened, yet Louis XIV is at odds with Pope
Innocent, who resents his encroachments on the Church's territory.
And while Innocent is mobilizing support to defeat the Turks, King
Louis is secretly hoping – even planning – that he will fail, so that he
and the Sultan can carve up what is left of the Habsburg empire. And
so we inch towards the discovery of a plot to poison the Pope.

Meanwhile, the apprentice has work to do. His boss falls ill and
he has to take over the cooking. His snacks and soups are thrown

together, then disguised with heaps of cinnamon. Naturally, the guests rebel. Food, as we know from our Covid confinement, is a source of comfort. Fortunately, the cellars of the *locanda* are stuffed with provisions kept cool in sacks and ice: wine, oil, fruit and vegetables, salted, smoked and dried meat; tongues, sweetbreads, tripe and other offal, game birds of all kinds, even swallows and sparrows; and more than thirty varieties of fish, shellfish, frogs and snails. These mouth-watering culinary treats are followed by eye-watering enemas administered by the resident doctor Cristofani who, with the boy, tours the house dishing out prophylactics and potions cooked up from outlandish recipes which he has learned by heart.

An important ingredient of the plot is the seductive rondeau played repeatedly by one of the lodgers, Robert Devizé, a French guitarist. Devizé (or de Visée) was a real person, as was Francesco Corbetta, the guitar virtuoso who composed the piece supposedly for Louis XIV's queen, Maria Theresa. The rondeau turns out to be a message in code, vital to the outcome not only of the power struggle in Europe but also of the battle for Vienna. To say more would be to say too much.

The rondeau reminds us that musical cryptography was familiar to the Renaissance and Baroque ages. We are in a period overshadowed by myth and magic, a time when alchemy and astrology were struggling to become 'science'. Experiment was all the rage. And so we are introduced to the German Jesuit priest and polymath Athanasius Kircher (1602–80), professor of mathematics at the Collegio Romano. Kircher was an intellectual magpie who studied everything from Egyptian hieroglyphs to magnetism, and who was obsessed with automata and other mechanical inventions. He wrote enormous, lavishly illustrated books to flaunt his own extravagant theories while shamelessly borrowing other people's work. But Kircher was not always wrong: he proposed, for instance, that bubonic plague was carried by infectious micro-organisms, even though he could not possibly have seen them under his microscope.

Imprimatur is a cunning combination of fact and fancy. A preface dated 14 February 2040, written by the purported Bishop of Como, a friend of the authors, warns the Vatican of the risks involved in canonizing Pope Innocent XI. He complains that the couple had sent him a typescript and then disappeared, and he pretends to be unsure whether the book is pure invention, largely true or merely plausible.

Before becoming journalists, Rita Monaldi had studied the history of religion, Francesco Sorti the musicology of the seventeenth century. Like good scholars, they have provided endnotes to their novel, detailing their sources. This would suggest they had originally planned to write an historical exposé and had switched to a fictional form instead. If so, it was a good decision. It doesn't matter what liberties they may have taken. Their story is both delightfully implausible and completely gripping, a jigsaw in which hundreds of apparently random pieces fit beautifully together to form a picture.

As for the local colour I had been counting on, there was little on offer. That's no surprise, given that we, the readers, are underground for half the time and locked in for the rest, emerging into the open only for a grand, cinematic finale. Monaldi and Sorti have written two sequels, *Secretum* and *Veritas*, which contain further exploits of the wily abbot Melani, but I haven't dared try them – a great act can be hard to follow.

CHRISTIAN TYLER, a retired *Financial Times* journalist, has not forgotten the advice once given him by Doris Lessing: if you want to learn about another country, don't buy guidebooks. Read its fiction.

Out with the Galloping Major

CAROLINE JACKSON

On one of my more recent trips to Ireland, I took a detour through County Waterford to visit Lismore Castle. Towering over the steep, wooded banks of the Blackwater, it was built nearly 900 years ago by an English prince, was once owned by Sir Walter Raleigh and has been the Irish seat of the Dukes of Devonshire since the eighteenth century.

The castle is a fairytale sight but what caught my eye, given pride of place on one distinctly ancient and sturdy-looking wall, was a plaque. Said wall, it explained, replaced one that had collapsed 'for no apparent reason'. No more, no less. I was, briefly, bemused; on reflection, quite the opposite. That precise phrase recurs, to pointed and poignant effect, in *Troubles*, J. G. Farrell's sublime tragicomedy about the dying days of Ireland's Protestant Ascendancy. As I sheltered from the rain, by now rather less soft than it's fabled to be, in the lee of that notable wall, it struck me as the perfect summation of the entire Anglo-Irish predicament.

I was on a pilgrimage to Castletownshend, the West Cork crucible of a unique and celebrated writing partnership, appreciation of whose work is one of my infallible yardsticks of congeniality. When not quite into my teens, I noticed that my parents were unusually

---

Somerville & Ross, *Some Experiences of an Irish RM* (1899), is out of print but we can obtain second-hand copies.

taken with a television series called *The Irish RM*, 'based on stories by Anglo-Irish novelists Somerville and Ross'. Broadcast in the UK in the early 1980s, when the IRA was committing some of its worst atrocities on the mainland, it was an early and, perhaps, surprising success for the then new Channel 4. More beggar than chooser, I settled down to watch with them and was soon hooked on the galloping misadventures of Major Sinclair Yeates who, as the eponymous Resident Magistrate, arrives in turn-of-the-century western Ireland fresh from his regiment and appointed by the Lord Lieutenant to administer justice; or so he hopes.

No one 'of Irish extraction' is born free of history but back then, in relative ignorance, I enjoyed the programmes as a simple period sitcom, squirming as Yeates (a perfectly cast Peter Bowles) was merrily disabused of the notion that his position commanded any respect from the horse-trading, hard-hunting and hard-drinking denizens of Skebawn (think Skibbereen) who are, it transpires, also hard-wired to outfox him at every turn.

That said, I couldn't fail to catch shades of my immediate family in this world of no tomorrows where the idiom rang familiar, and complex snobberies went hand-in-glove with that peculiarly Irish disdain for 'mock swank' or delusions of grandeur. It was, however, some years before I actually read any of the original *Irish RM* stories; when I did, so much suddenly made sense.

Edith Somerville of Drishane House, Castletownshend, and her second cousin Violet Martin (always 'Ross', after her Galway home) were introduced in 1886 at Somerville's large and convivial home, the hub of a seaside village crowded with extended family, all ferociously talented and pathologically busy. By the standards of the day, neither was in her first flush ('we were, as we then thought, well stricken in years . . . not absolutely the earliest morning of life; say, about half-past ten o'clock, with breakfast (and all traces of bread and butter) cleared away'). From that moment, neither looked back.

Somerville had been born in Corfu where her officer father was stationed but by the age of 27, when she met the woman who was to become her professional partner and soul-mate, this avowed spinster ('I'd love to be an ould maid. A single life is airy.') was not only an accomplished musician and horsewoman but also unusually well-travelled, a positive Home-ruler and determined – by necessity as much as conviction and having trained in London, Paris and Düsseldorf – to make her living as an artist ('I will paint. I will also work.'). Ross, four years younger but already a published writer, arrived into this 'clanging heronry' from a far quieter nest of gentlefolk. Reduced to penury – and staunch Unionism – by unpaid rents, the Martins were one of the Tribes of Galway whose estates had once extended to over 200,000 acres.

Both hailed from that elusive breed best understood in terms of its loyalty to the English crown but variously described as the Ascendancy, hyphenated-Irish or, with the contempt indulged in by those deeming themselves authentically Irish, West Britons. Survivors of successive English plantations dating back to Elizabeth I but in retreat since the 1800 Acts of Union and beleaguered by absenteeism, Catholic emancipation and land reform, they were the tenacious 'horse Protestants' of propaganda (who were, ironically, to furnish many of the prime movers of the emergent Free State). Knowing this centaur class from within, the pair soon set about immortalizing its fugitive charms.

They began with a 'Buddh' dictionary (Buddhs being all descendants of their common great-grandfather, the 'silver-tongued' former Lord Chief Justice of Ireland, Charles Kendal Bushe). Vital for 'situations in which the English language failed to provide sufficient intensity', it gives a flavour of the cousins' shared eye for pretension, ear for speech and incorrigible nose for absurdity:

Minaundering pres. p. of verb used to describe the transparent
   devices of hussies (deriv. from the Fr. 'minauder' translated as
   'to mince, to simper, to smirk').

Medear n. Method of address – seldom implying affection.
White-eye n. A significant and chilling glance calculated to
awake the fatuous to a sense of their folly.

It was a short step to their first novel (*An Irish Cousin*, 1889) but one
hard fought. Penelope Fitzgerald, an ardent admirer, was indignant on
their behalf that they were 'treated as the joke of the family' when, for
their part, they consciously looked back to Maria Edgeworth for example, commending her 'sincerity' and sharing her 'privilege' of 'living in
Ireland, in the country, and among the people' of whom they wrote. By
the time Lady Gregory boasted of being 'the first to write in . . . *the English of Gaelic thinking people*', they were already busy 'eavesdropping':
'Ireland has two languages: one of them is her own by birthright; the
second of them is believed to be English, which is a fallacy; it is a fabric
built by Irish architects with English bricks, quite unlike anything of
English construction . . . *expressing with every breath the mind of its
makers*.' Pastiche was anathema (neither had much truck with the Cel-
tic Revival and its efforts to mythologize a heroic past). What inspired
them was their own, dwindling microcosm of ordered chaos.

Seven novels later – including *The Real Charlotte* (1894), which
V. S. Pritchett rated the best Irish novel of any period – Somerville
and Ross embarked on a collection of short stories entitled *Some
Experiences of an Irish RM* (1899) as a riposte to a London editor's
sneer about 'an overdose of Ireland'. This was followed by two more
collections, *Further Experiences of an Irish RM* (1908) and *In Mr Knox's
Country* (1915). Written in the middle of those fraught three decades
between the loss of Charles Stewart Parnell – champion of Home
Rule – and the Anglo-Irish Treaty of 1921, the stories tackle the im-
passe between occupier and occupied in a spirit of irreverent fatality.
Politics and religion flicker (officials from Dublin Castle and nationalist Catholic clerics both get short shrift) but the tales derive their
finest comedy from class conflict as much as racial difference, blithely
comparing a terminal situation to 'a gigantic picnic in a foreign land'.

In each, the animating crisis is always in prospect but its form and degree are anyone's guess. Narrated by the hapless Major Yeates – like Bertie Wooster, a Magdalen man – there's never a dull moment nor the slightest hope that he'll prevail over the self-serving machinations of his landlord and fellow member of the bench, Flurry Knox ('a stableboy among gentlemen and a gentleman among stableboys'); Flurry's redoubtable grandmother, old Mrs Knox ('a rag-bag held together by diamond brooches'); his housekeeper Mrs Cadogan ('a name made locally possible by being pronounced Caydogawn' and borrowed, tongue firmly in cheek, from the reigning Viceroy); or Flurry's mendacious groom Slipper. Even Yeates's game and sprightly wife, Philippa, is reduced to stitches at her husband's expense by all but the most dire and muddy predicament.

Throughout, all parties are, by and large, gleefully complicit in the farce afoot, typically involving untimely exits and entrances, wayward animals and copious liquor. The prevailing shamelessness and unsentimental witness to the tooth and claw of country life – framed by exquisite descriptions of Ireland's wild beauty and rendered in pitch-perfect vernacular – would be easy to confuse with condescension. Instead, calamity after calamity testifies to 'the inveterate supremacy in Ireland of the Personal Element' (a mantra to which, in the story *'Poisson d'Avril'*, Yeates nobly clings through mounting vicissitudes involving a dead salmon). No one should be surprised when Slipper the groom, 'with the manner of the confederate who had waded shoulder to shoulder with me through gore', tenders the following advice: 'It's hunting you should be, in place of sending poor divils to gaol.'

Forget Wilde's quip about the unspeakable in pursuit of the inedible. You barely need to know a hoof from a halter to appreciate the genius with which this pioneering pair captured 'the unsuspected intoxication of fox-hunting'. Until the fall which precipitated Ross's premature death in 1915, both were addicted to the chase. It was perfect fodder for breakneck sagas such as 'The Pug-Nosed Fox' in which Yeates, installed as Deputy MFH in Flurry's absence ('Be fighting my grandmother for her subscription, and whatever you do, don't give more than half a crown for a donkey. There's no meat on them.') finds himself separated from the field and not only supernumerary at a wedding feast, a feast just demolished by his pack, but even proposing the toast . . .

As with Wodehouse, nominating a favourite is as impossible as analysing the stories' magic but 'Trinket's Colt' exemplifies what Somerville later defined as 'the art of being jolly in creditable circumstances'. Hold hard as Flurry – bent on turning a profit on his grandmother's prize foal – inveigles Yeates into a little light larceny, fortified by 'sherry that . . . would burn the shell off an egg'. Culprit and stolen colt have just found themselves eyeball to eyeball in a furze-fringed, sandy grave when Mrs Knox heaves into view.

To Somerville – who continued to write under their joint names until her death in 1949 – their collaboration was 'like blue and yellow which together make green'. Ross dubbed it their 'Irish eye'. Not for them the anxiety Elizabeth Bowen described feeling 'English in Ireland, Irish in England'; but they would not have disputed her claim that in relation to Ireland 'no fiction could improve upon or exaggerate reality'. The Irish RM stories can get lost in translation, mistaken for rather suspect caricature. That's precisely the point. The joke falls on the impecunious Anglo-Irish as much as it appears, at first glance, to be at the expense of the 'native' Irish, its edge all the keener for the deep and never-to-be-admitted sympathy between them. Somehow, they make lasting sense of a vanished world and remind me, somehow, of that inscrutable plaque.

CAROLINE JACKSON read English at Oxford but was brought up to believe the best English is spoken in Dublin. She now lives in Cambridge and spends her days looking west to where the grass is definitely greener.

Poetry, My Mother and Me

RACHEL KELLY

My mother Linda Kelly was a historian and lover of the eighteenth century, with biographies of Sheridan, Tom Moore and Talleyrand to her name. Though I studied history at university, when it comes to my own writing, my subject matter has been rather different – books on mental health and wellbeing, including a memoir about my own experience of depression, and a cookbook about eating with your mood in mind. But we had one literary overlap: I have always loved poetry and so did she. I think we both found it easier to communicate through the words of others. Poetry was our common ground.

We had very different upbringings. A child of the Thirties, she grew up in Hampshire, in a comfortable mock-Tudor house covered in Virginia creeper. She belonged to the post-war stiff-upper-lip generation. I remember her telling me admiringly that her father never spoke about his wartime experiences. To me the implication was that she found it best to avoid talking about anything too personal or emotional.

By contrast, I grew up in Notting Hill in the 1970s and loved chatting about my feelings. She rarely opened up in return. Other people's poems were the safe place where we met, and in the poems she recommended I glimpsed something of her own rich interior emotional life.

When I had my heart broken as a teenager, she gave me 'Apple Blossom' by Louis MacNeice, with its lines:

> The first blossom was the best blossom
> For the child who had never seen an orchard.

There would be other blossoms, other love affairs. She knew what I was going through. More than that: she too had known the agony of young love rejected.

Then, in my last year of university, a friend died. She sent me Ben Jonson's poem on a life cut short, with its verse:

> A lily of a day
> Is fairer far in May,
> Although it fall and die that night –
> It was the plant and flower of Light.
> In small proportions we just beauties see;
> And in short measures life may perfect be.

That last line meant a lot to us both, I felt. A few months before my friend's death, my father had been struck down by a stroke which left him semi-paralysed. My mother's life would never be the same again. She effectively became his carer for the next thirty years. She knew only too well that 'in short measures life may perfect be'.

Reynolds Stone

I remember too the moment in my late twenties when I realized how intense her love was for us children in her choice of William Blake's 'Infant Joy', which she gave me when my first son Edward was born.

> I have no name
> I am but two days old. –
> What shall I call thee?
> I happy am
> Joy is my name, –
> Sweet joy befall thee!

I hugged the poem tight, knowing that she was signalling not just the delight she felt at the birth of her first grandson, but also her own delight when she had become a mother, and indeed her profound love for us three children. This was something of which she rarely spoke – unlike many of my generation who say 'love you' to their offspring in every passing text.

Perhaps the deepest poetic communication between us was during my thirties when I fell ill with serious depression. I was in need of poetic consolation, and my mother was a rich source, for she knew literally hundreds of poems off by heart. Her richly stocked mind came to my rescue. Lying in bed, I was a child again as she recited poems to me or read to me from her own private collection. It turned out that all these years she had, in a battered red leather book, been squirrelling away snippets of poetry, prayer and anecdotes that had particularly struck her.

I drank up the collection as if it were ice-cool water offered to a parched traveller. Towards the end of her life my mother decided to publish it. In the introduction to *Consolations: A Common Place Book*, she wrote: 'The collection has always been for my own consumption but recently I lent it to one of my daughters who was suffering from depression and she found it so comforting that I thought it might be a source of consolation – or interest or amusement – for others too.'

Poetry helped me in lots of ways, not least in dissolving the feeling of solitude. Others had suffered – among them the poets themselves. And of course, as the months passed, the extent to which my mother had also suffered slowly dawned on me. While she had not succumbed to clinical depression, inevitably the themes of loss and pain had played through her life. I only wish now that I had asked her more about her own dark nights of the soul. I think we shared the feeling that the poets had made something of their suffering, reordering the seemingly random cruelty of illness into some kind of sense.

Poetry absorbed and revitalized us both. Its condensed nature and sophisticated vocabulary required a concentration that shocked us into the moment in an almost physical way, freeing us from worries past and future. Because of course she was worried too – that her daughter might not recover.

We began with short poems, many of which are dotted through my memoir of that time, *Black Rainbow*. One favourite was 'New Every Morning' by Susan Coolidge. It particularly helped at the painful start of the day and was better than any pep talk my mother might have given me about the virtues of a positive attitude:

> Every day is a fresh beginning,
> Listen my soul to the glad refrain.
> And, spite of old sorrows
> And older sinning,
> Troubles forecasted and possible pain,
> Take heart with the day and begin again.

Later, as my concentration improved, we turned to the seventeenth-century poet George Herbert. When she read the first verse of 'Love (III)', I felt a sudden shock of recognition.

> Love bade me welcome; yet my soul drew back,
> Guilty of dust and sin . . .

The idea that my soul was 'guilty of dust and sin' seemed the perfect description of depressive illness. The poem pinpointed a sense of guilt that I should be depressed even though I was blessed with a loving home, husband and children, feelings of shame that I had not previously acknowledged. Yet love wins through. Now I wonder more what my mother's own psychological struggles had involved. Needless to say, we never discussed them.

My mother chose the poem for her funeral, and I recited it that day at St Mary of the Angels in Bayswater. It is the only poem I can recite without a smidgen of worry that I could ever forget a line or a verse. I often recite it now when I am awake in the small hours, comforted by the thought that the poem was one to which my mother had turned.

Later, when I had recovered from the worst of the depression in my early forties, I edited a children's poetry anthology, dedicating it to my mother who had first instilled a love of poetry in me. After so many years of receiving poems from her, I had begun to slip poems her way. I developed a passion for Emily Dickinson. Knowing my mother's love of small birds, and the trials she faced nursing my father, I gave her 'Hope is the Thing with Feathers'. Doubtless she already knew it. But by giving her a copy, I hoped that she knew I recognized her sacrifice and her need to keep on keeping on.

One of my last memories of her was in the hospital dialysis unit, a windowless, airless room, attached to a machine she didn't want to be attached to. Desperate to distract her and make light of how miserable things were, I searched for 'The Lady of Shalott' on my phone. It was one of the first poems I had ever learned by heart, something we had done together, me lying on the beaten-up olive-green sofa in our sitting-room, she pacing the room with *The Oxford Book of English Verse* and correcting my mistakes. I had mostly forgotten what I once knew of the poem, so now I read aloud to her from the bright white of my screen, as once she had read to me. I think I was trying to say thank you, for nurturing my own love of poetry and the rich poetic inheritance she had passed down to me. And to thank her for everything really.

RACHEL KELLY is a writer and mental health campaigner. She is an ambassador for SANE and Rethink Mental Illness.

Bibliography

Richard Altick, *The Scholar Adventurers*   24

Anita Brookner, *Hotel du Lac*   65

Mary Soames (ed.), *Speaking for Themselves: The Personal Letters of Winston and Clementine Churchill*   73

George Clare, *Last Waltz in Vienna*   13

Hugh Falkus, *The Stolen Years*   34

William Golding, *The Spire*   7

Doris Lessing, *The Four-Gated City*   19

Brian Masters, *Killing for Company*   60

Rita Monaldi & Francesco Sorti, *Imprimatur*   79

Poetry: the consolation of   90

Charles Ritchie, *The Siren Years*   43

Somerville and Ross, *Some Experiences of an Irish RM*   84

John Squire (ed.), *Cheddar Gorge*   54

Rosemary Sutcliff, *Sword Song*; *The Shield Ring*   39

Josephine Tey: the Inspector Grant novels of   49

J. R. R. Tolkien, *The Hobbit*   69

Mary Wesley: the novels of   28

Coming attractions

MORAG MACINNES receives some post from Hudson Bay · ANDREW RYAN takes up the sweet science · SUE GILD goes by sledge to Siberia · MATHEW LYONS heads for Broadway with Damon Runyon · LAURIE GRAHAM eavesdrops on the Windsors · DAISY HAY spends a year in Barsetshire · MARTIN EDWARDS eats some poisoned chocolates · PAULINE MELVILLE bumps into a ghost in Guyana

THE STORIES OF ENGLISH

DAVID CRYSTAL

AFTERWORD BY THE AUTHOR

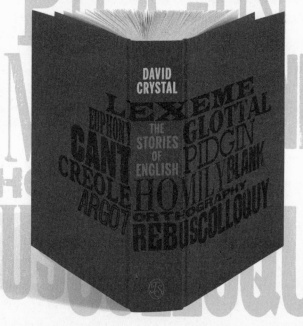

 The Folio Society